God's Venturer: HUDSON TAYLOR

Hudson Taylor, aged 21,
just before he left for China.

GOD'S VENTURER

HUDSON TAYLOR

by
Phyllis Thompson

CHINA INLAND MISSION

LONDON . PHILADELPHIA . TORONTO
MELBOURNE . THUN . CAPE TOWN

First published 1954
Reprinted December 1955
Reprinted May 1958
Reprinted November 1960

Made in Great Britain

Published by THE CHINA INLAND MISSION,
NEWINGTON GREEN, LONDON, N.16,
AND PRINTED BY THE CAMELOT PRESS, LTD.
LONDON AND SOUTHAMPTON

Trade Agents: THE LUTTERWORTH PRESS
4 BOUVERIE STREET, LONDON, E.C.4

CONTENTS

CHAPTER ONE

THE LAST HALF-CROWN

IT was past ten o'clock on a dark night, and the raggedly dressed man accompanying him was a complete stranger. Nineteen-year-old Hudson Taylor fingered his one remaining half a crown to make sure it was still in his pocket, and looked around him rather apprehensively. He had been along these poor, narrow streets before, and even in broad daylight they were not inviting. Now, with street lamps flickering feebly at the corners of dark alleys, and suspicious-looking people slinking into doorways, the neighbourhood looked anything but safe and respectable. It was certainly not the sort of place one would choose to walk in with ragged strangers after dark. But, after all, if he was going to China he must no doubt get used to this sort of thing, so he went on.

"Why didn't you ask a priest to come and pray with your wife?" he asked his companion, rather glad to hear the familiar sound of his own voice! The man had come to him with the story that his wife was dying. "Will you come and pray for her soul?" he had requested, and Hudson Taylor had readily agreed. Now, however, he was beginning to wonder. The man was evidently a Roman Catholic. If his wife were indeed dying, why had he not obtained the services of a priest, of whom there seemed always an adequate supply in this Irish quarter of Hull? Why come to a Protestant?

The man explained. He had been to the priest. The priest, however, had demanded one shilling and sixpence down before rendering his services. And as he and his family were starving already, and had no money left at all, a fee of one and sixpence for a prayer was quite out of the question.

Starving! Hudson fingered his one remaining half a crown uneasily. It was all he had; apart from two bowls of porridge in his lodging he had neither food nor money. He could scarcely be expected to part with that one remaining coin. He felt unreasonably annoyed with the man, and reprimanded him severely for having allowed things to get to such a pass. Why had he not gone to the Poor Law officer, and asked for help? A dying wife and a starving family, and doing nothing about it, indeed!

"I went," replied the man dismally. "He told me to come back to-morrow morning at eleven. But my wife, she be dying. She'll be gone before morning, I'm fearing. . . ."

Hudson's heart was touched. His own position had seemed precarious enough, but how much worse was the lot of his companion. If only his half a crown were in two shilling pieces and a sixpence, he thought to himself, how gladly would he have given him one of the shillings!

The man turned suddenly out of the street, and into a dark courtyard. Hudson had been here before, and he remembered the last occasion very distinctly. He had been buffeted and pommelled by the indignant slum-dwellers who had torn up the tracts he gave them, and bade him begone. If ever he shewed his face here again, let him beware! The priest with his crucifix and prayers to Holy Mary was welcome enough, but not a young English Protestant preacher, begorrah! Hudson had departed with what dignity he could muster, little thinking he would ever be invited to return. And as he felt his way gingerly up a rickety flight of stairs in one of the tenement houses, he sincerely hoped that his presence would not become widely known in the area! He was quite relieved when they reached the top of the stairs and he heard his companion open a door. They had reached their destination.

What a sight met his eyes! The dim light from a cheap, guttering candle revealed bare boards, curtainless window, and a room almost devoid of furniture. On the floor in a corner, lying on a straw mattress was a thin, exhausted woman, and beside her a new-born baby, not yet two days old. Standing around, or lying on the floor, were four or five other people—children in ill-fitting clothes, without shoes or stockings, who looked towards their father and the stranger he had brought with him, with large, listless, hungry eyes.

Hudson stood silently in the room, acutely conscious of his half a crown. Oh, if only it were in two separate shillings and a sixpence, he thought. Certainly he would immediately produce one of the shillings *and* the sixpence, and give to these poor people. But it was no use wishing. He pulled himself together, remembered that he was a preacher and intended being a missionary, and decided he must tell these people about God.

"You know, things are very bad for you just now," he faltered. "But you mustn't be cast down. We have a Father in heaven Who loves us and cares for us, and if we trust Him . . ."

The words seemed to stick in his throat. "Hypocrite!" something inside him seemed to say. "Telling these people about a kind and loving Father in Heaven—*and not prepared to trust Him yourself*, without your half a crown!"

Hudson gave up trying to preach. The family looked at him in silence, as he stood there before them in his long-tailed coat and wide wing collar, wearing real leather shoes and with a top hat! What if his clothes were getting threadbare, and his shoes needed mending? Compared with them he appeared wealthy beyond their dreams. How were they to know he only had half a crown left in the world? Hudson felt very depressed indeed. Oh, if only that half a crown were a florin and a sixpence, he would give them the florin, he really would, and keep only the sixpence for himself! But it wasn't a florin and a sixpence. . . .

He turned to the man, and said: "You asked me to come and pray with your wife. Let us pray now." It would be easy to pray, he thought, as he knelt on the bare floor. But it wasn't. No sooner had he commenced "Our Father Who art in Heaven," than that accusing voice within said again, ". . . that half a crown in your pocket." He pressed through his prayer, feeling more and more miserable, and then rose to his feet.

And as he did so, the man said to him in desperation: "You can see what a terrible state we're in, sir. For God's sake, help us!"

Poor Hudson! There was nothing for it now. He remembered suddenly something he had read often enough in the Sermon on the Mount. "Give to him that asketh of thee. . . ." Give. . . .

Slowly he put his hand in his pocket. The half a crown, all of it, would have to go.

"You may think I'm well off," he said to the man, as he handed him the coin. "But as a matter of fact, that's all the money I've got in the world." Surprisingly, he began to feel quite cheerful. "But what I've just been telling you is true, you know. God really is a Father, and we can trust Him. *I* can trust Him. . . ." And he realized he could. He found himself speaking with great assurance and confidence about trusting God, now that the half a crown was out of his pocket and in the man's! He was amazed at the difference it made to his feelings. He was positively buoyant now. He and the family parted from each other, with mutual expressions of good will, he made his way down the rickety stairs and out into the court-yard, walking home with his head in the air, coat tails flapping jauntily, singing at the top of his voice, without a care or a penny in the world! And when he reached the small bed-sitting room in Drainside where he was lodging, and prepared to eat his last but one bowl of porridge, he felt as happy as a king.

An interesting thought occurred to him as he sat there. He remembered that he had read somewhere that "he that giveth to the poor lendeth to the Lord." It put that half a crown in quite a different light to feel that, having given it to some poor people, he had merely lent it to God. The idea of lending God half a crown might seem rather startling, but as it was in the Bible he knew it was all right. So when he knelt to say his prayers before going to bed, he mentioned the matter of the loan, requesting that it might be replaced soon, otherwise he would have no dinner the next day!

The following morning he arose as usual, and looked at his last bowl of porridge. A hard day's work lay before him, and while one good bowl of porridge was enough to start on, it was scarcely enough to continue on. When would God repay that loan?

He sat down and commenced eating. The postman's rat-tat-tat was heard on the front door, but he paid little attention, since he rarely received letters on Monday mornings. But within a few seconds his landlady appeared at his door.

"Here's a little package for you, Mr. Taylor," she said cheerfully, holding it towards him in her apron, for her hands were wet.

"Oh—thank you!" replied Hudson, rather surprised.

He took it from her, and looked at it. It was addressed to him all right but he certainly did not recognize the writing. The postmark was blurred, so that did not help him, either. He decided to open it. Slitting open the envelope, he drew out a sheet of paper. Inside was a pair of kid gloves.

"Whoever is sending me kid gloves?" he thought, mystified, as he opened them out. And then something fell out. It was a very small object, and it gleamed. He stooped to pick it up—it was a golden half-sovereign.

He stared at it in amazement; looked through the paper wrapping for a letter; scanned the handwriting and the postmark for a clue as to who had sent it. All in vain. He never discovered where it came from. And at that moment he did not really care. As far as he was concerned, it had come straight from Heaven! It dawned on him that not merely had his half a crown been returned, but three more besides. Suddenly he laughed aloud.

"That's good interest!" he exclaimed jubilantly. "Ha! Ha! Half a crown invested in God's bank for twelve hours brings me in ten shillings! This is the bank for me!"

CHAPTER TWO

DRAINSIDE

D RAINSIDE, Hull, where Hudson Taylor had come to live, was so called for the excellent reason that it was beside a drain. Officially the drain went by the name of canal, but to the people living in the rows of tiny cottages built on either side of the narrow ditch, it was just a drain. Very convenient it was, too, to the inhabitants of those cottages. By merely opening their front doors and throwing hard they could dispose of all their rubbish without giving themselves any further trouble. Dirty paper, cabbage leaves, potato peelings and rotten vegetables floated about on the water unashamed, providing admirable targets for street urchins to throw stones at. And if the drain exuded unpleasant odours, and proved a danger after dark to those who emerged unsteadily from the public house opposite which Hudson lodged, its advantages as an ever-available dust-bin more than compensated for these minor defects.

To Hudson the contrast between this poverty-stricken, unattractive area and the beauties of the Yorkshire town near the Pennine Range from which he had come, was sharp indeed. How different, too, was his shabbily-furnished little bed-sitting room from the cosy, comfortable home over his father's chemist shop in Market Square, Barnsley! The warm parlour behind the shop, with its dresser of gaily coloured china and sparkling glass, its large book-case, and comfortable sofa and chairs seemed a palace to the little room with a bed in one corner, and a table and a couple of chairs as the only furnishing, in which he now lived. It was lonely, too, eating his frugal meals in solitary state, instead of sitting down to a well-spread table with his parents and two chattering younger sisters. He enjoyed teasing those sisters, with their corkscrew curls and frills on their frocks, and he missed them—especially Amelia. But it was in order to get accustomed to loneliness and hardship that he had come here, and he was determined to stick it. It was part of his preparation for living in China.

Ever since the December evening more than a year previously, when he had heard a Voice saying to him "Go for Me to China" he had known that he must go. He was praying at the time when he heard that Voice, and although China had not been in his thoughts at all, the command was so clear and unmistakable that he had no doubt it was from God. It was because of his determination to obey that he had left his congenial home at Barnsley to come and work for a doctor in Hull. A little medical knowledge and experience would be useful in a strange land, he decided, and this move to Hull was but the first step in his journey towards that far-away Empire of the East.

Not only was he anxious to gain medical knowledge as his equipment for life as a missionary in China, however. That was a small matter compared with another question which constantly confronted him. He knew no one in China, and he was going alone. Was his faith in God strong enough for him to go to a strange land and face difficulties and dangers hitherto unknown?

"When I get out to China," he thought, "I shall have no claim on anyone for anything. My only claim will be on God. What if my faith isn't the right sort? Supposing my prayers don't work?" And the more he thought about it the more he realised that he must learn to move men through God, by prayer, before he left England.

To move men through God, by prayer. The thought gripped him. Could it be done? Hudson wanted to find out. And in a very simple, natural way, the opportunity to try it out was presented to him—through his employer.

Dr. Robert Hardey was a friendly, kind-hearted, vigorous man with a never-failing fund of good humour. It was said he made people laugh so much they were cured of half their ailments without any medicines at all! With a large practice and many claims on his time, he was too busy to attend much to business details, and one day he said to his young assistant:

"Taylor, please do remind me when it is time for me to pay you your salary. I'm so busy, you know. I'm quite likely to forget. . . ."

He did forget. The time came when he was due to pay Hudson, and nothing was said. A day or two passed, and still no reference was made to the matter of his salary. And Hudson was faced with two alternatives. He could ask the doctor for the money, or he could ask God. And remembering that when he got to China he would have no one to ask but God, he decided to ask Him now. That was why he was down to his last half a crown on the Sunday night when he gave it away to the starving family. Little wonder that when the golden half-sovereign fell out from the mysterious packet the very next morning, he laughed aloud for joy! Here was adventure indeed! He'd taken a risk to find out whether it worked, this idea of trusting God, and it *had* worked! Right in the nick of time the money had come, and God alone knew from whom. Hudson certainly did not. All he knew was that he had not gone without a single meal through trusting God, although it had looked very much as though he might, as he sat eating his last bowl of porridge. He felt like Elijah must have felt when the ravens arrived with his dinner!

"It works! It works!" Hudson sallied forth from his lodging, golden half-sovereign in pocket, light-hearted and jubilant. Trusting God worked! Obeying God worked! It was a wonderful life, stimulating, exciting! Hudson might have been walking on air, so happy was he.

However, he realized that half a sovereign would not last for ever. The main problem still remained—the payment of his salary. The cheerful, busy doctor might go on for months without remembering it, and the question was, would God remind him?

Daily Hudson prayed that the doctor might remember, and then went cheerfully on with his work and study, confident that something would happen. A week passed, and his ten shillings was diminishing slowly. Three shillings out of it for his rent made quite a hole, but he had sufficient to last him until Saturday—but after that. . . .

Saturday came. The doctor said nothing. The day wore on, until by five o'clock all the patients had been attended to, and the doctor came into the dispensary where Hudson was boiling up some medicine, and sitting down in his arm chair started to talk. Evidently he had no thought of the salary, and Hudson, carefully watching the mixture in the pan, made no reference to it. Then, quite suddenly, the doctor said:

"By the by, Taylor, isn't your salary due again?"

Hudson gasped. After all, it was all right! Once more, when down to his last coin, the necessary money was coming! He gulped once or twice before replying quietly:

"Yes, as a matter of fact, it was due two or three weeks ago. . . ."

"Oh, I am so sorry!" exclaimed the doctor. "Why didn't you remind me? You know how busy I am. I do wish I had thought of it a little sooner, for I sent all the money I had to the bank only this afternoon. Otherwise I would pay you at once."

Poor Hudson! The sudden dashing of his hopes was almost too much. It was as though a bucket of icy cold water had been thrown over him. Fortunately, the concoction in the pan he was watching boiled up, and he rushed with it from the room, glad for an excuse to get away. But when he was alone, he threw himself on his knees. His disappointment was so great he could scarcely pray coherently. What his prayer lacked in coherence, however, it made up for in earnestness, and after a while he calmed down. Indeed, somewhat to his surprise, he found himself feeling quite cheerful again. God would certainly work for him, he thought hopefully, and although he had no money at all to pay his landlady her three shillings when he returned to his lodging, even that knowledge did not unduly depress him.

It was late when he prepared to leave the dispensary that evening. The hands of the clock had ticked slowly round until they stood at about ten minutes to ten when he started to put on his overcoat. "Well, my landlady'll be in bed by the time I get back," he thought. "So I shan't have to see her this evening and tell her I can't pay the rent this week—that's good!" He walked over to the gas bracket, preparing to turn it off, when he heard the sound of footsteps outside. It was the doctor, and he was laughing heartily, as though greatly amused.

"Why, hello, Taylor, are you still here?" he exclaimed. "What do you think? One of my patients has just come round to pay his bill! He's one of the richest patients I've got, and he could have paid me by cheque any time. Yet here he is, bringing the money round at ten o'clock on a Saturday night!"

Hudson laughed. That a man rolling in money should

come round himself to pay his doctor's bill at such a time was certainly unusual. What had possessed him? People were not usually so punctilious about paying doctors' bills!

The doctor made his entry in the ledger, and started back towards the door, when suddenly he turned.

"By the way, Taylor," he said. "You might as well take these notes. I have no change, but I can give you the balance of your salary next week. . . . Good night."

And Hudson, his pockets empty, was left standing in the dispensary with a hand full of bank notes. His prayer was answered. Not only could he pay his landlady, not only had he money in hand for weeks ahead, but he had proved again that God answered prayer! There was no question about it now—he could go to China.

CHAPTER THREE

ONLY A PIN PRICK

MRS. FINCH, Hudson's landlady in Drainside, was married to a sailor who, as is the way with sailors, was usually away at sea. His wife had a hard time to make ends meet on his small allowance, and very glad she was to have the doctor's young assistant lodging in her front room for three shillings a week. That was all she had to pay for the rent of the whole house, and as he gave no trouble, she considered herself very fortunate to have him! Her lodgers were not usually such respectable, considerate young gentlemen as this one, and when one day he broke the news to her that he would be leaving she was genuinely distressed.

"I'm going to London to attend a medical course in the London Hospital," he explained.

"Well, sir, very sorry I'll be to lose you," she said. "You're going to London . . . ?" That gave her an idea.

"I wonder if you would do something for me while you are there," she asked. Certainly he would if he could. Then she explained. Half of her husband's pay was sent to her from the shipping offices in London each month, and a charge was made for sending it. If Mr. Taylor would kindly collect the money from the offices and send it to her instead, he would save her quite a lot of money.

Hudson, of course, readily agreed to do this, although when he got to London he discovered it involved a long walk in the middle of the day to fulfil the commission. And as he had a four-mile walk from his boarding-house to the hospital each morning, and a four-mile walk back each evening, he was scarcely in need of any further exercise!

This move to London to take a medical course was a big thing to him. He was already in touch with a very small mission called the Chinese Evangelization Society, which was prepared to send him to China as a missionary, and with the approval of this society he was now embarking on further medical training. It was as definite a step towards the land of his desire as the move to Hull had been, and had been taken at a risk of which he spoke to no one.

The risk was again along the lines of testing his own faith, and his own ability to endure hardships. His father had offered to supply him with the money necessary to live in London and take the medical course; the Chinese Evangelization Society had made a similar offer. After duly considering the matter, however, and praying about it, too, he decided to accept neither. He thanked his father and said that he would not need his help, and his father naturally thought he was receiving his support from the missionary society. He thanked the board of the missionary society and said he would not be needing their help, and they thought he was receiving his support from his father! And so he arrived in London one very foggy day with the few pounds he had saved, not knowing what would happen when they were spent.

He was determined to learn to trust God to meet his needs as they arose. At the same time, he felt he must live as economically as possible. It had been arranged that he should share an attic bedroom in Soho with a cousin of his, and this he was glad to do. Far better to live with a friendly relative than be entirely alone in the great city. He bought his own food, and here he was indeed economical—he spent about threepence a day! After a few experiments, he had decided that brown bread and apples, with clear cold water, was the most inexpensive diet he could find! So on his way to the hospital he bought a pound of apples for his dinner, and on his way back, passing warm-looking restaurants from which emanated provokingly appetizing odours, he called in at a baker's shop and bought a twopenny brown loaf.

"Will you cut it in half, please," he requested of the baker. And with the two halves under his arm he continued his long walk home, and climbed the three flights of stairs to his room. One half of the loaf provided him with his supper, and the other half was resolutely put aside for breakfast—however hungry he felt.

"No, my health does not suffer," he wrote to reassure his mother, who was anxious about him. Was he getting proper food, she wondered? Had she but known! "On the contrary, everyone says how well I look, and some even that I am getting fat! Though this," honesty compelled him to add, "can only be perceived by rather a brilliant imagination!"

It was about three months after his arrival in London that he received an urgent letter from Mrs. Finch. Would he, she requested, be so kind as to draw her allowance for her as soon as possible? Her rent was nearly due, and she had no other money with which to pay it.

The request had come at an awkward time for Hudson, for he was studying diligently for an examination, and spent every spare minute over his books. Rather than take the time to go all the way to Cheapside, it would be better to send the money out of his own diminishing supply, and call at the shipping office to collect the remittance after he had taken the examination. This he did, little dreaming of the stormy seas that awaited him. For when eventually he went to the shipping office, the clerk told him he could not have the money!

"The officer Finch has run away from his ship," he said, "and gone to the gold diggings. . . ."

"That's rather inconvenient for me!" exclaimed Hudson, somewhat taken aback. "I've already advanced the money to his wife! She'll have no means of repaying me, I know."

"I'm sorry. Very sorry indeed," said the clerk. But there was nothing he could do, of course, and Hudson departed.

After the first shock, he was not unduly perturbed. After all, he thought, he was out to trust God to provide him with what he needed, as soon as his own funds were exhausted. This only brought that time nearer. Indeed— as he counted over his remaining coins he realized that the time was very near indeed! The memory of his Drainside experiences encouraged him, however, and he returned to his attic feeling cheerfully confident that all would end well.

During the evening he made himself a notebook. It was cheaper than buying one. He selected some sheets of paper, fitted them together, and started sewing them when he accidentally pricked the forefinger of his right hand. It was only a prick, and in a few seconds he had forgotten it. But that prick nearly cost him his life.

The following day at the hospital he had the task of assisting in dissecting the body of someone who had died of fever. It was not only a disagreeable task, but a dangerous one as well. The students had been solemnly warned that the slightest scratch on their hands, should it become infected, would probably prove fatal, and they all worked carefully, avoiding anything that might cause an abrasure in their skin. When Hudson, therefore, began to feel inexplicably weary, and then was suddenly sick, it did not occur to him that there was anything seriously wrong with him. He was merely surprised, since his diet was not of the type conducive to bilious attacks! He drank a glass of cold water, felt a little better, and went to a lecture. But his right arm began to pain him so acutely that he could not write. The pain spread to his side, and he felt really ill. He could not go on like this.

"I can't think what has come over me," he said to the surgeon in the dissecting room.

"Why, what's the matter?" he enquired. Hudson tried to describe how he was feeling, and the surgeon, looking at him keenly, said, "What has happened is clear enough, I fear. This is a case of malignant fever. You must have cut yourself while you were dissecting."

"No, sir, I'm sure I didn't. I haven't got a scratch or a cut. . . ."

"Well, you certainly must have had one," said the surgeon. "Let me look at your hand." While he was doing it, Hudson remembered the prick of the needle the night before. Could it be that, he asked? Yes, the surgeon thought it might well be.

"You'd better get a hansom cab and drive home as quickly as you can," he said gravely, "and put your affairs in order." He looked at the young medical student, from whom it was useless to try to disguise the gravity of the situation.

"For," he said bluntly, "you are a dead man."

CHAPTER FOUR

STRENGTH THROUGH PRAYER

HUDSON'S first reaction to the doctor's startling pronouncement was one of sorrow and disappointment. If he were dying, that meant he could not go to China. China! How he had longed to go there! How deep had been his conviction that God had a work for him in that land! It seemed impossible that he had been mistaken about it all. And then the thought came—*had* he been mistaken? If God really intended him to go to China, thought Hudson, then he must get better, in spite of the doctor's assertion that there was no hope.

This he endeavoured to explain. He was not at all afraid to die, he pointed out. Indeed, the prospect of being with His Master, whom he was learning to love very much, was a very inviting one. However, he was sure he had a work to do for Him in China first, and therefore he must be pulled through this illness.

"That's all very well," the doctor rejoined impatiently. This was no time for the young student to reason why he should live, when it was evident he was going to die! "You get a hansom and drive home as fast as you can. You've no time to lose. You'll soon be quite incapable of winding up your affairs. . . ."

It was scarcely a cheering motive for hurrying, and, furthermore, he had not enough money to pay for a four-mile ride in a hansom cab. Hudson smiled a little wryly to himself as he departed. He dragged himself slowly along the road to the place where he could get on an omnibus, and wearily mounted it, conscious of the pain in his arm as the clumsy vehicle rumbled and bumped along the streets. When at last he reached his lodging and climbed slowly up the three flights of stairs to his attic, he was exhausted. Thinking, however, to improve his condition, he lanced his finger to let out some of the poison. The pain was intense—and that was the last thing he remembered. He fell unconscious to the floor.

*   *   *

For some weeks Hudson lay in his bed, too weak to move from his room. When he had been found in a dead faint on the floor, an artist uncle of his who lived nearby had been called, and this kindly man had taken charge of him, sending immediately for a doctor, despite Hudson's protestations that he could not afford to pay the bill.

"He is my own medical man, and the bill will be sent to me," he said reassuringly. "Don't worry over that." But when the doctor arrived and heard Hudson's story, he looked grave.

"Well," he said frankly. "If you've been living moderately, you may pull through. But if you've been going in for beer and that sort of thing, I'm afraid there's no hope. . . ."

With vivid memories of apples and brown bread washed down by cold water, Hudson was able to reassure him on that point! If recovery depended on having avoided high living, he knew of no one who stood a better chance!

"But now," said the doctor. "It's going to be a hard struggle. You must do everything possible to keep up your strength. A bottle of port wine every day, and as many chops as he can eat!" he told Hudson's uncle. Hudson had little taste for that sort of diet, but he did his best with it, and after many days and nights of suffering he was at last able to move out of his room and lie for an hour or two on a sofa in the boarding-house parlour. It was not until then that he learned that two other medical students who had become infected about the same time as he were both dead. Why had his life, then, been preserved? He felt it could be for no other purpose than that there was a work for him to do in China.

One day when the doctor came, after expressing satisfaction at the progress made by his patient, he said:

"The best thing you can do now is to get off to the country as soon as you feel fit to take the journey. You must rest until you have gained more strength. If you start work too soon, the result may still be serious."

When he had gone Hudson lay back on the sofa to review his position. "Get off to the country." His thoughts flew to the cosy, happy home in Yorkshire; the Cudworth road along which he had raced so often as a child, merrily bowling his hoop, and teasing Amelia as she came trotting breathlessly behind, corkscrew curls a-bob; the shady glades of the Lunn Woods, where butterflies fluttered, and birds' nests could be found; the distant view of the Pennines. "Get off to the country." The doctor's order was wholly attractive, and commended itself to both heart and head! Hudson realized that he was still far too weak to attempt the strenuous life in the hospital yet, and obviously there was nowhere where he could regain his health so quickly as in his own home. There was only one obstacle in the way—he had no money at all for the fare.

Actually, as he well knew, the money could be obtained with the utmost ease just for the asking. His kindly uncle would undoubtedly be more than willing to forward it. And were he to drop the veriest hint in a letter home, his fare and more would be forthcoming by return of post. But as he lay on the sofa, exhausted as he was after the exertion of walking down the stairs, there was something in him that refused to consider taking the easy and obvious course. He still wanted to try out this method of getting used to relying on God to answer his prayers, instead of depending on the people who certainly would not be at hand to help him in China. He closed his eyes as he lay there and, explaining this to God, asked Him what he should do.

After this prayer he remained quiet for a while, thinking over the matter. If he had not forwarded that money to Mrs. Finch, he thought, he would have had ample. And if only Finch had not elected to desert his ship at that particular time, he would have been able to draw the money. Then the thought came that perhaps if he went to the shipping office he might yet be able to draw it. Although it seemed most unlikely, since he had forwarded the remittance to Mrs. Finch entirely on his own responsibility, the thought persisted.

Was God putting it into his mind, he wondered. Or was it just a silly idea of his own? He was not sure. So he closed his eyes again and prayed, asking God which it was. Because if the idea did come from God, the fact remained that the shipping office was two miles away, and he had not the money needed to ride there! To walk, of course, was simply out of the question. It had been necessary for someone to help him even walk down the stairs! Yes, to walk was out of the question—but was it? *Was* it? To his own surprise, Hudson found himself thinking, that perhaps it was not out of the question, after all. God had already done some quite remarkable and unexpected things after he had prayed. Jesus Christ had said, "Whatsoever ye shall ask in My Name, that will I do, that the Father may be glorified in the Son." He had said it eighteen hundred years before, but as Hudson lay in the boarding-house parlour, it all seemed suddenly real and up-to-date. There was something very convincing about that calm assertion. "Whatever you ask in My Name, I will do it." In view of it, to walk to the shipping office in Cheapside no longer seemed out of the question. Obviously all that was necessary was to ask to be strengthened to do it. So that is what Hudson did. Then he rang for the boarding-house servant, and asked her to go up and fetch his hat and stick; and having had them handed to him by that respectful but somewhat surprised damsel, he slowly emerged from the boarding-house, and turned along the quiet street into the busy thoroughfare leading towards the City.

His progress, admittedly, was slow. He displayed an altogether unwonted interest in the contents of shop windows, pausing at almost every other one to lean against the glass. Ladies in crinolines swept past him as he continued his deliberate, leisurely pace, and street vendors cried after him to buy their wares in vain. He did not so much as turn his head to watch an elegant coach with briskly trotting horses come smartly along the street— indeed, it is doubtful whether if the young Queen Victoria herself had driven past he would have roused himself to look. But gradually the way was traversed. He had asked for strength to walk it, he reminded himself as he faced the sharp incline that led to Cheapside, and strength would surely be given—walk it he did. He arrived safely at the shipping offices and sat down on the steps before attempting to climb the stairs up to the first floor. It was a little unusual, he realized, to take a seat just there. The top-hatted gentlemen who hurried past him, up and down the stairs, evidently thought so, too. They eyed him with some surprise, as though thinking, "Tut, tut! Quite a respectable looking young fellow, too. . . !" However, no one spoke to him, and eventually he climbed the stairs and entered the office.

This was the crucial moment.

After all the exertion of the two-mile walk, was he to be met with a disappointment? But somehow Hudson felt it was going to be all right. And it was! The clerk who greeted him recognized him immediately.

"Oh, I am so glad you have come," he exclaimed. "It turns out that after all it was not the mate Finch who ran away, but an able seaman of the same name. I shall be glad to give you the half-pay due to Mrs. Finch up to date. It will no doubt reach her more safely through you than through her husband. His ship has just reached Gravesend, and we all know the temptations these men meet when they come ashore after a voyage." He looked keenly at the young medical student, standing so pale and obviously weak. "But before I give you the money," he continued "You must have a rest and something to eat. I'm just going to have my lunch. You must come inside and share it with me."

Gratefully Hudson accepted the kind invitation, and glad enough he was of the opportunity to rest as well as eat! He took his journey back to Soho in an omnibus, too! He could afford it now! But the effort he had made seemed to have done him good rather than harm. The next morning he felt so much better that he had no hesitation about going round to the doctor's surgery to settle his bill. His uncle had already done so much for him, he was unwilling to leave him to pay it and spend his own money on railway fares to take himself home for a holiday. And although he realized that by paying the doctor's bill himself he would almost certainly be left with insufficient money to buy his ticket, it seemed the only honourable thing to do. To the doctor, therefore, he betook himself. And there a further pleasant surprise awaited him. The doctor refused to charge him anything.

"You're a young medical student," he said firmly. "As such, I shall charge you nothing for my services."

"But medicines. . . ." remonstrated Hudson. "All that quinine. I ought to pay for that."

"Very well," said the doctor. "Quinine. We'll say eight shillings for the quinine, and that's all."

Eight shillings! Hudson made a rapid mental calculation as he handed over the surprisingly small sum. When his bills were paid, there would be just sufficient left for his railway fare to Yorkshire, the omnibus journey to his home, and the necessary food for the journey! He was overjoyed. This was wonderful! At every step he found his affairs were planned out to what seemed perfection. He simply could not keep it all to himself, this amazing evidence that God was fully prepared to take responsibility for the ordering of his life. And if for his, most certainly for others, too. The doctor must be told.

"Pardon me, sir," he said respectfully. "But I wonder if you will allow me to speak to you freely, without being offended. I feel that under God I owe my life to your care and attention, and I am truly grateful. And there is something I want to tell you about. . . ." Whereupon he related the whole story of his reason for being in London, his intention to find out if God really answered prayer before he went to China, and the things he had experienced in doing so. The surgeon listened with kind, though sceptical interest until Hudson told him of his walk to Cheapside the previous day. But that he could not believe.

"Impossible," he exclaimed. "Why I left you lying on that sofa looking more like a ghost than a man!"

"I did walk it, indeed, sir," asserted Hudson, explaining

that he had prayed in the Name of Jesus to be strengthened to do it, before starting out.

"Do you mean you walked—you did not go by hansom
cab, or even by omnibus?"

"No, I walked."

"All the way from Soho to Farringdon Street, and then
up Snow Hill to Cheapside. . . ?"

"Yes, sir. . . ."

The doctor was interested now. It seemed incredible
that one who had been so weakened by illness could take a
two-mile walk alone through London's busy streets, and
be none the worse for it. He listened to the recital of the
happy outcome of the walk in the money received, how
Hudson had been able to settle all his bills, and last of all,
that after the eight shillings for quinine was paid, he had
just enough in hand to see him home. There was a
restrained yet evident joy about the convincing way
Hudson told his story that touched the older man's heart.
This practical confidence in a God who, after all, could
neither be seen nor heard, was something new to him.
Unaccustomed tears welled slowly up in his eyes as he
looked at the strangely radiant expression of the open-
faced boy before him, and he said in a voice deepened by
emotion:

"I'd give all the world for a faith like yours."

"You can have it, you know, sir," answered Hudson
quietly. "It's free to all—without money and without
price."

CHAPTER FIVE

HOME AGAIN

THE horse-drawn omnibus rattled over the cobbles, and came to a standstill in Market Square, Barnsley. The passengers emerged one by one, and eventually Hudson appeared, somewhat tired and travel stained after the long journey from London. How friendly and familiar everything appeared—how good it was to be welcomed back home by his strict yet genial father, be-whiskered and coat-tailed, and by the gentle mother with her smoothly brushed hair and dainty muslin cap tied under the chin. And how pleasant, as he walked out, stick in hand, for a stroll, to be greeted warmly by this friend and that, glad to see him again, and eager to hear of his life in the far-away capital. It was all so different from London, where he was just an unimportant stranger, and walked along the busy streets with never a greeting from anyone to cheer him. Weak as he still was from his illness, home was the place above all that afforded him complete rest and satisfaction. He sat contentedly by the fire in the warm parlour behind the shop, glad of the old familiar setting that brought back so many happy memories. What scenes were revived by the sight of the large, sturdy table in the middle of the room, for instance. Once more he was a very small boy, dressed in his best velvet suit, sitting at the table surrounded by visiting grown-ups. He was watching his mother cutting a delicious looking apple pie into generous portions, which were handed along to her guests—indeed, to everyone but her own small son, who sat politely silent, as he had been trained, waiting in vain for the plate that was intended for him! Came the realization that somehow mother had overlooked him this time —and he had been told that on no account must he *ask* for anything at the table! The story of his ingenuity had passed down into the annals of family history as it was recalled, time and time again how, during a lull in the conversation, a little voice had enquired:

"Mamma—do you think apple pie is good for little boys?"

It was at that table, too, that he had sat, day after day, learning the lessons his father set for him, until eventually at the age of eleven, he went to school. Much happier he had been under his father's tuition than at school, too, though he was one of the star pupils there. There was something eminently wholesome and manly about this father of his, with his rigid ideas of right and wrong, and his unyielding discipline. Hudson had learned to be punctual long before he had his life ruled by clanging school bells! Woe betide the one who was not ready to sit at table, hands washed and hair brushed, when it was time for a meal!

"If there are five people, and they are all kept waiting one minute, then five minutes are lost," father would say sternly, adding slowly, "Minutes that can never be found again!" It was very solemn indeed!

"Learn to dress quickly," was another of his axioms. A very good reason he had for it, too! "For you have to do it once at least every day of your life." So, obviously one might as well get used to it! If Hudson smiled at these memories as he sat in the cosy home, it was with the affectionate amusement with which children are wont to view the idiosyncrasies of parents. And it was interesting to remember that it was from his father he had first heard of China when, as a little five-year-old, he had heard him exclaim vehemently:

CHT

"Why don't we send missionaries there! That is the country to aim at, with its teeming population . . . strong, intelligent, scholarly people!"

And now, nearly fifteen years after, Hudson himself was preparing to go there! As he spent those weeks at home, with plenty of time to think, he marvelled at the way his destiny had been revealed to him. For surely this was his destiny, the particular work that was appointed for him to do? "Go for Me to China." He could never forget the night when he received that Divine commission. Only one other experience, perhaps, stood out more vividly in his memory. China had not come into it, that afternoon in the old warehouse when his whole outlook on life had been completely changed, but had it not been for what took place then, certainly he would have no thought of going to China now. Many a time Hudson lived through that momentous afternoon again. It was over three years ago, yet as clear in his mind as if it had happened yesterday. . . .

He was sixteen years of age, and already disappointed with life! How dull it seemed, living here at home, and helping his father in the shop! It was not that he did not love his parents, for he did, but he found their manner of life irksome. Balls and hunting parties found no place in their programme. They preferred singing hymns in the little chapel down the road, and Hudson, dutifully accompanying them, thought it very dull indeed. He tried his best to enjoy it all as they did, but he could not. His own private desire was to live in a large house with a number of servants, from which he could sally forth, clad in a scarlet jacket, to go hunting. He longed to possess that which would enable him to rush along at the greatest possible speed—a horse, of course, motor cycles not yet having been invented! These desires, however, could evidently not be satisfied, and it was in a discontented frame of mind that he wandered into the parlour one afternoon in June, looking for something to do.

He glanced through the bookcase, but saw nothing there that appealed to him, so turned his attention to a basket of small, paper-covered books, and picked out one of them.

"I know what this will be," he thought. He knew the sort of paper-covered booklets his father was fond of collecting! "It will have an interesting story to begin with, and a moral or a sermon at the end." Well, he decided, he would read the interesting story, and leave the rest! So he took it off to the warehouse across the back yard, where he would be undisturbed by younger sisters with ideas for games and sat down amongst the boxes and bottles to read it.

He little knew that at that very moment his mother, on holiday about seventy miles away, was kneeling beside her bed, praying for him with unusual earnestness and intensity. Nor had he any idea that six weeks previously his thirteen-year-old sister Amelia had determined that she would pray for him three times a day until his mind was changed about God. That was what he needed—a change of mind about God. He had told her that he was not really at all sure about God; and very moody he seemed as a result! He wasn't even sure there was a God! Not sure there was a God! Amelia, being herself quite sure about God, felt this state of affairs must not be allowed to continue. Realizing, however, that her arguments, convincing and conclusive as they appeared to her, did not so seem to him, she came to the conclusion that only God could change Hudson's mind. That is why she determined to pray three times every day, until it happened. She even made a note of her decision in her diary. For all her corkscrew curls and frilly frocks, Amelia was a young person of some determination, and pray three times a day about the matter she did!

Unaware of all this, Hudson sat in the warehouse and read the booklet. It was the reading of that little booklet that completely changed his outlook on life. Quite suddenly and unexpectedly it dawned upon him that what he had heard about God and Jesus Christ from his earliest childhood, was true. God was real. Jesus Christ was His Son, and had died for the sake of sinners. He had come to life again, and was up there in Heaven alive, able to see everything on earth—able to see him, right there in the warehouse! He had died for the sins of the whole world—therefore He had died for the sins of Hudson Taylor. He had promised eternal life to all who believed on Him—therefore He had promised eternal life to Hudson Taylor. He heard prayer, therefore He would hear Hudson Taylor's! What a remarkable thing that, having heard it so many times before, it had only just dawned on him! Somehow, it made Hudson feel as he felt when he suddenly saw the simple solution to a mathematical problem that had puzzled him for hours—relieved, enlightened, exuberant. Everything was different now. The heavy feeling of discontent, the uneasy sensation of having done something wrong that would one day be found out, were gone. He felt free. It seemed too good to last!

But it did last. Three and a half years later, sitting contentedly by the glowing, crackling fire, Hudson knew that it lasted. The years since that June afternoon had not been idle, easy ones—indeed, they had contained certain trials and hardships hitherto unknown. But there had always been the exhilarating consciousness of adventure in an unseen realm. The stimulation of finding out that God answered his prayers, that God would lead him into unexplored pathways he would never have discovered himself, was far greater than that of galloping along after the hounds in the limited environs of Barnsley and district! And he knew the simple secret of getting rid of that sensation of guilt. He merely did what he knew to be right, and when he inadvertently did that which was wrong, he confessed it to God, who has promised to forgive when sin is acknowledged! Yes, it lasted!

The weeks at Barnsley sped past all too quickly, and renewed in health and spirits, Hudson faced London again. Not without many a pang did he bid farewell to the intimate warmth and love of home. He was beginning to know from personal experience what it meant to tread a lonely pathway, and to endure weakness and privation without the sustaining comfort of like-minded companions. But after all, that was the way to grow strong and self-reliant. Pioneer missionary work required *men*—not molly-coddled weaklings! Hudson, delicate from childhood, was determined to be a pioneer missionary—and therefore he must be in every sense of the word, a *man*.

His parents, however, not unnaturally, were distinctly averse to his becoming a man if doing so involved return-ing to a diet of apples and brown bread, washed down by water. Indeed, they had grave doubts as to whether he would ever become one that way—even Hudson himself agreed the matter was open to question! Instead of residing in the Soho boarding-house and buying his own food, it was decided he should obtain a position as doctor's assistant, where he could live with the family. This he did. He attended lectures at hospital in the morning, assisted his surgeon employer from dinner-time until nine o'clock in the evening, and the rest of the day was his own—he could start studying for lectures then!

It was a strenuous life, certainly, but he was happy. Good food and a comfortable home did make a difference to his spirits, he found! And during the next six months he gained not only much useful medical knowledge and experience of human nature, but further evidence of that which he knew to be of even greater importance—the help God would give in all matters about which he prayed.

One outstanding example was the case of the man with gangrene. A thoroughly hardened drunkard he was, and now he lay dying, though he did not know it.

"It's no use speaking to him about religion," Hudson was warned when he visited the home where the man lodged. "He's an atheist. He won't hear a thing about religion. We asked a Scripture reader to come and visit him once, and he got in a towering rage and ordered him out of the room." The Vicar of the parish had called, too. Alas, he was forced to depart in some confusion, for the infuriated invalid only permitted him to advance near enough to spit in his face! Hudson felt not unlike a gladiator entering the arena when he called for the first time to dress the man's foot. Speak to him about God's willingness to forgive his sins, and to receive him as the father received the prodigal, he must. Why, the man was dying! What hope was there for him in this world or the next, without God? But Hudson decided to wait a propitious occasion to broach the all-important subject. Until the angry and rebellious attitude had in some measure altered, it would be worse than useless to do so. He took special care in dressing the man's foot therefore, and said nothing about religion for several days. But the man was on his mind. He felt responsible for him, and many times a day Hudson prayed for him. "Learn to move men through God by prayer." If his prayers for the softening of hard hearts did not prove effective here in England, he could scarcely expect to be successful in heathen China.

Gradually the man's attitude changed. It changed first of all towards Hudson. The young medical student dressed his foot so carefully and skilfully that the pain was considerably eased, and he felt really grateful. Indeed, he went so far as to say so! This, surely, was the opportunity for which he had waited, thought Hudson. He explained to the man how he trusted in God to help him in all his medical work, and then went on to the subject of everyone's need of God's forgiveness and mercy.

Had he been the Scripture reader or the Vicar, he would probably have fared as they did! However, as he was the doctor, and as such able to relieve his pain, the man managed to swallow his wrath, merely expressing it by turning his back without a word, and remaining there, with his face against the wall, until Hudson departed! It was not exactly encouraging, but at any rate it was a step in the right direction. The next day Hudson broached the subject again—with the same result. And after several more visits, his heart began to sink. Was it any use continuing? It seemed not. One day he felt so discouraged, so anxious about the man who, despite his ill-temper, was so often in his thoughts, that he felt something rising in his throat, and tears came to his eyes.

"Oh, friend, you must listen!" he exclaimed, and walked towards the bed. "Oh, if only you would let me pray with you!" and he found himself speaking in a broken voice, expecting the man to turn his back as usual. But the man did not. He looked with surprise at the overwrought young doctor who was obviously so upset about something, and said:

"Well, if it will relieve you to do it, you can!"

It was scarcely a warm invitation, but Hudson needed nothing more. He knelt down, closed his eyes, and prayed aloud. Oh, that God would open the eyes of the dear man!

Oh, that he might know that God was real, that Jesus Christ had died to save him from the punishment due for his sins, that forgiveness was his for the asking. The man lay silent, and although he made no comment then, it was evidently the real turning point in his life. No longer did he turn his back when Hudson spoke to him about God. The realization was dawning on him that what this earnest young man repeatedly told him was true. And if it were true—why not believe it? Why not . . . ? And so it came about that one day Hudson left his patient's room almost walking on air. The erstwhile bitter, hardened old man, who had not been inside a church for forty years, and then only to get married, was lying in bed, his eyes reverently closed, learning to pray to his God.

CHAPTER SIX

STORM AT SEA

THE ship was moving. The gangway had been removed after the friendly mate, the last man to leave the shore, had jumped aboard, and now, slowly and silently, the ship was leaving the dock-side. Hudson stood alone on deck, waving to the little group of people standing watching him depart. His eyes were fixed upon his mother. Dear, gentle, stalwart little mother! She had tried so hard to be brave, but down in his cabin, when she had been gently smoothing the bed-clothes on his bunk, he had caught her with tears on her cheeks, and just now, after she had said the last goodbye and left the ship, she had sat down quickly on an old piece of timber, as though she were going to faint. Hudson had run down the gangway to her, and given her a last, reassuring hug.

"Don't cry, mother dear," he had said. "It is only for a little while. We shall meet again. . . ." But he had to hurry back on board and leave her. She was standing up now, her full skirts billowing in the breeze, waving her handkerchief to him. Hudson, loath to lose sight of her, suddenly turned and climbed up into the rigging, to get a better view. Standing there among the swaying ropes he held on firmly with one hand, and with the other waved his hat vigorously. It would cheer her up, perhaps, to see him like that! High above his head the sails were flapping and the masts creaking as the ship drew towards the dock gates. The beloved figure on shore seemed to be getting smaller and smaller, and her little fluttering handkerchief more minute. . . .

"Oh-h-h!" Hudson stopped waving at the sound of that piercing cry. It was his mother. The ship was passing through the dock gates now, and making for the open sea, bearing her only son away to that distant, unknown land —China! This was goodbye indeed! The anguish of that cry went through Hudson's heart like a knife. What this was costing her! She was suffering so much more than he! A lump rose in his throat.

The ship was gathering speed now, and he could no longer distinguish the little figures standing at the end of the dock. He strained his eyes, peering through the misty air until he knew he could see them no more, and slowly swung down on to the deck, the sound of that cry still ringing in his ears. A new thought was submerging his mind. If it cost his mother so much to see him leave her for China, what must it have cost God to part with His Son, when Jesus came to earth to die for man's sin? Was not God a Father? Was not Jesus "His only begotten son"? Somehow, the sacrifice of parting that he and his mother were feeling so keenly seemed to bring him nearer to God, to understand better what was meant by the love of God. God loved, so He knew what this sort of suffering was, too. Hudson felt strangely strengthened in the midst of his pain as he went down to his cabin.

He was the only passenger on the *Dumfries*, a small sailing ship of only 470 tons, and he had been told it would be five or six months before it would dock in Shanghai. In 1853 there was no Suez Canal route to the Far East, and the little ship must breast its way through the waves around the Cape of Good Hope, and brave the typhoons of the Pacific before it could reach its destination. A long sea voyage indeed, and one that provided him with enough danger and excitement during the first ten days to last him the rest of the trip! Almost as soon as the *Dumfries* entered the Irish Channel she had to make her way in the teeth of a gale, and for days she was driven hither and thither like a cork, by the force of the winds. Hudson had never known anything like it, and rapidly revised any ideas he may have had about the romance of a sailor's life. The timbers creaked and groaned, sea water found its way into the cabins, his clothes felt damp and sticky, and as the days and nights passed, the storm seemed to increase in fury until on Sunday afternoon the seas were mountainous.

Hudson struggled up on deck, and clinging to the side of the ship, looked around on the wild scene. The sea was white now with foam, and waves came rolling, one after another, until they seemed to tower above the little *Dumfries* like threatening cliffs as it floundered in a trough of swirling water. When it seemed that it must be submerged, then the vessel would begin to tilt dangerously, and Hudson, feet sliding on the slippery deck, could scarcely keep his balance until the ship perched dizzily on top of the liquid cliff only to plunge down again as the wave rushed on. As he looked across the raging seas, he saw a large ship astern, beaten along by the winds, and a little brig. How helpless they all were, and how powerless they would be if the waves dashed them together!

The captain was standing beside him, face set and anxious. Never had he seen a wilder sea, he admitted.

"Unless God helps us," he added solemnly. "There is no hope."

"How far are we from the Welsh coast?" asked Hudson. The dangerous Welsh coast with its rocks jutting out into the sea!

"Fifteen or sixteen miles. . . ." But they were drifting towards it, for the west wind was blowing. "We must carry more sail. The more sail we carry, the less we shall drift.

God grant the masts can stand it. . . ." What if they were
to snap under the strain of the wind? But the risk had to be
taken. Their lives were at stake. He ordered two sails to be
hoisted.

The ship plunged forward, faster than ever, with the
wind filling the sails. It was rolling one-sidedly, with the
waves at times rushing right over the lee bulwarks. The
evening was drawing on, and the sun was sinking behind
a bank of clouds. Hudson watched it solemnly.

"To-morrow thou wilt rise as usual," he thought, feeling
rather dramatic. "But unless a miracle happens, all that
will be left of us will be a few broken timbers floating on
the waves. . . ." How his family would sorrow if he were
drowned! And what a waste of money for the Chinese
Evangelization Society, who had spent about £100 on his
outfit and passage! And what would it feel like, that
struggle in the raging waters before they finally closed over
his head? It was a melancholy thought. Hudson felt cold
and lonely and rather frightened in the gathering
darkness, with the wind roaring and the spray beating
into his face. He fumbled his way slowly to the gangway
and descended into his cabin. Finding his hymn-book
and Bible, he sat on his bunk and started to read.

"Let not your heart be troubled; ye believe in God,
believe also in Me. . . ." There was such a calmness about
the familiar words, that somehow he began to feel calmer
himself. He read on, and after a while, his eyes tired with
reading in the uncertain light of the swaying lantern, he
threw himself on the bunk and fell asleep.

When he awoke, it was approaching midnight. The
ship was still pitching violently, and the wind roaring.
How far were they now from land, and those treacherous
rocks? Hudson went up on deck again. Peering across the
moonlit waters, he saw a light ahead. It was the Holyhead

lighthouse, sending forth its warning to all ships that might
be approaching too near. The Holyhead lighthouse—
and the rocks. . . .

"Can we clear it?" he shouted to the captain, the sound
of his voice almost carried away by the wind.

"If we make no lee-way we may just do it," the Captain
shouted back. "But if we drift, God help us. . . ."

And they did drift. Helplessly they watched the light
to which they were drawing nearer and nearer. How long
would it take the ship to reach it, drifting at this rate?

"Have we got two more hours?" shouted Hudson.
Probably not so long, was the reply. Less than two
hours. . . .

Hudson went down to his cabin again, the tears starting
to his eyes as he thought of his father, his mother, his
sisters. Never to see them again on this earth! How they
would grieve, not knowing what had happened to him
when the ship went down. He took out his pocket-book
and carefully wrote in his name and address. If his body
were found, that would identify him, he thought. That
provision having been made, he looked around for means
to save himself from drowning at all. He had not given up
all hope of survival. Seeing a hamper which he thought
might float, he decided to take it up on deck, and hold on
to it tight when the ship went down. He put a few things
in it which he thought might be useful if he ever got to
land, and struggled up on deck again.

All the time, in his heart, he was praying. He found it
almost impossible to frame coherent sentences, for his
mind was in a turmoil, but something within went on
mutely beseeching God, his Father, to save them. He
looked at the sea, and saw the waters white with foam in
the bright moonlight. Only a few hundred yards ahead of
them, it seemed, was land, and the rocks.

"Can the boats live in a sea like this?" he asked the captain, wondering why they were not lowered.

"No. . . ."

"Couldn't we lash some spars together and make a raft of it?" suggested Hudson.

"No time. . . ." The captain moved suddenly, as though he had made up his mind.

"We must try and turn her, or its all up," he said. They seemed to be making straight for the land that lay just ahead. "We'll have to tack. . . . The sea may sweep the deck in turning, and wash everything overboard . . . but we must try!" and he gave the order. The effort to turn the ship outward failed. The force of the wind and the waves was too strong. Desperately the captain turned the ship the other way. It meant sailing dangerously near the rocks, but with the added impetus of the wind in the sails, it was just possible they might be cleared. All eyes were on those rocks, with the white foam dashing against them and splashing feet high into the air. Could the ship steer clear? They were only two ships' length away, and if the little vessel could not hold her course, she would be dashed to pieces within a few minutes. Breathlessly Hudson watched, clinging to the rigging as the ship, tossed up and down, beat her way through the waves. They were passing the rocks! They were passing—they'd passed! Now, could they but beat out to sea, away from that dangerous coast, they might yet be saved.

Then it happened. The wind that had been beating so relentlessly on them, veered in their favour. The change of direction was only slight, to be sure—a mere two points—but it was sufficient to carry them away from the coast at last. When the sun rose on Monday morning it shone down, not as Hudson had feared, on a few broken timbers, but on a little vessel, sails gallantly hoisted, making for the open sea!

CHAPTER SEVEN

ARRIVAL IN CHINA

AFTER the excitement and danger of those first days, Hudson was thankful indeed when the ship entered warmer and calmer climes, where his belongings, saturated with salt water, at last got dried. For weeks that ran into months the little *Dumfries* sailed the oceans, first the Atlantic as she travelled down the west coast of Africa, right across the Indian Ocean to within 120 miles of Australia, and through the straits between the islands of South-east Asia, leading to the Pacific. It was among those islands that Hudson learned the dangers of being becalmed can be as great as those of being driven by the wind!

For days the sails of the little ship had been hanging limply from the masts, with scarcely a breeze to stir them. On more than one occasion she had progressed only seven miles in 24 hours, and in spite of the interest of seeing palm-fringed islands on the horizons, or watching the tropical fish that darted through the waters, the voyage was growing tedious. It was nearly five months since he had come on board at Liverpool, and Hudson knew every rope and every plank on the deck of the *Dumfries*. Heartily glad would he be to set foot on dry land again!

One Sunday morning, as he was conducting a service on deck, he noticed that his good friend, the captain, looked worried. He paid less attention to the service than was usual, and every now and then walked over to the rails, looking out across the smooth waters. There was not the slightest breeze and when, a little later, the crew had dispersed, and Hudson was standing alone with the captain, he learned the reason for his anxiety. The ship was being carried along by a strong current towards some sunken reefs, and without a wind to fill the sails, there was no way of resisting the power of the waters.

"We are so near the reefs already, that I doubt whether we shall get through the afternoon in safety", the captain told him. At sunset a breeze usually sprang up, but by that time the ship would probably be floundering hopelessly on the jagged, hidden rocks. The only possible hope lay in lowering one of the boats, and endeavouring to tow the ship out of danger. All the efforts of the men, rowing furiously, were in vain, however. The current was too strong, and they could not so much as turn the ship's head.

The captain stood beside Hudson in silence, and then said in as matter-of-fact a voice as he could:

"Well, we've done everything that can be done. We can only wait now. . . ."

Quite suddenly, Hudson thought of something. If only the breeze that usually blew up at sunset blew up *now* they, would be saved. And although they had no power at all over winds and breezes—God had. God could make the breeze blow earlier.

"There is one thing left that we haven't done," he said quietly.

"Oh? What is that?" queried the captain.

They had not prayed. That was the one thing left that remained undone. The captain was silent, and Hudson continued. There were four or five of them on board, out of all the crew, who believed in God and believed that He heard prayer. "Let each one of us go to our cabins, and let us all agree to pray that God will send a breeze *now*. He can send it just as easily now as this evening. . . ."

The captain was a little surprised at the suggestion,

but after a momentary hesitation he agreed. Very well, he said, they would do that. He would go to his cabin and pray, and Hudson could find the mate, the steward, and the Swedish carpenter, and suggest that they do likewise. They, of all the members of the crew, were known to be God-fearing men. Let them do the one thing left that could save the ship.

Hudson had been in his cabin praying but a short while, when he felt so certain that God was going to send a breeze that he got up from his knees, went on deck, and suggested to the first officer that he let down the corners of the mainsail.

"What would be the good of that?" asked the first officer scornfully. Not unreasonably, he felt he knew more about the time to let down sails than the young "land-lubber" before him!

"We have been asking God to send a wind," explained Hudson, "and it's coming immediately!"

The first officer fairly snorted.

"I'd rather see a wind than hear about it," he retorted forcefully. But instinctively he glanced up towards the sails, and Hudson, following his gaze, saw the corner of the topmost sail flutter.

"Look at the royal!" he exclaimed excitedly. "The wind is coming!"

"It's only a puff!" said the officer unbelievingly. He shouted an order, nevertheless, and within a minute barefooted seamen were thudding across the deck, and up into the rigging. The sound of the sudden activity brought the captain up from his cabin to see what was happening. And there were the sails, billowing in the breeze, while the ship turned slowly and steadily from the reef to cruise away at six or seven knots! And there was young Hudson Taylor, his eyes gleaming with joy and his heart brimming over with thankfulness, quietly rejoicing in his God, who answered prayer.

It was less than a month later that the *Dumfries* eventually anchored at Gutzlaff Island to await the coming of the pilot who was to guide them up the estuary to Shanghai itself. The sunny skies and blue waters of warmer climes were left behind now. Instead, as he stood by the rails, Hudson saw nothing but a thick fog and the dull, sullen-looking waters of the mighty Yangtze, the river that carves its relentless way from the mysterious tableland of Tibet through the fertile, populous plains of China to empty itself at last in the turbulent China Seas.

Hudson peered around him, straining his eyes for a glimpse of the land to which he had come. The fog was too thick to afford him a view of the long, low-lying shore yet, but as he leaned over the rails he discerned the dim out-lines of other vessels—strange-looking craft with one enormous sail hanging from the mast, and with curved, curiously painted hulls. There was no mistaking them for anything else but the Chinese junks whose pictures he had studied so often in the illustrated book on China in the old home at Barnsley! Now he was seeing them with his own eyes, and as he watched one drew near enough for him to see the men on board. Loose-fitting blue home-spun jackets and trousers, skin the colour of old parchment, dark, enigmatic eyes, long thin hair plaited in a pigtail— Chinese! For the first time Hudson looked into the faces of members of the great race to which God had sent him, and amongst whom he expected to spend his life. He could not understand a word of their language, and their strangely inexpressive faces betrayed nothing of their feelings. How could he set about learning to speak, he wondered. Where would he go to live when he went ashore on this unknown land? How, indeed, would he even get anything to eat, since he had no idea what to ask for! He paced the deck, muffled in his warmest clothes, revolving these and other questions in his mind until his reverie was interrupted by the sudden activity on deck.

"The pilot! The pilot's coming aboard!" What excitement! For the first time in five and a half months here was someone who could give them news of the outside world! For the first time in five and a half months, here was another Englishman mounting the gangway! It seemed that everybody on board came on deck to see him. And what news he had to give them. In the five and a half months in which they had been sailing the oceans, cut off entirely from the outside world, troubles had arisen in Europe which were leading up to war. In China itself was war already—civil war, with great Rebel forces sweeping up from the south against the Imperialist armies that poured down from the north. And what affected Hudson most vitally was the fact that Shanghai itself was right in the thick of the fighting! Rebels held the city, which was besieged by an Imperialist army of about fifty thousand men. Food was already at famine prices, and the rate of exchange was rising. An English pound sterling, which would previously buy five Chinese dollars, would now only purchase three!

Little wonder that the next day it was with very mixed feelings he stepped ashore, and followed his guide through swarms of vociferating, shouting Chinese coolies, to the British Consulate. He was in China at last! That was thrilling. But as he picked his way across the mud, he could not but be aware of the difficulties that confronted him. No one was expecting him, he had not one friend in the whole of Shanghai, and he had very little money. He had three letters of introduction to people living in Shanghai, however, which he planned to present as soon

as possible. Apart from that, he had no idea what he ought
to do, now he had arrived at last! The dangers of the sea
voyage suddenly seemed insignificant compared with the
extreme sense of loneliness that now assailed him. And on
arrival at the Consulate, the replies to his enquiries after
the men to whom his letters of introduction were addressed
only served to intensify his distress.

The first man, he learned, had died of fever a month or
two previously. The second had already returned to
America. Only the third was known still to be in Shanghai
—and the letter of introduction to him had been given
Hudson by a comparative stranger! It was with a sinking
heart he set off to the compound of the London Missionary
Society.

He walked for over a mile through streets which got
narrower and narrower as he left the European quarter
behind. Curved roofs, overhanging balconies, tiny, dark
little shops with ornate, swinging signs, all seemed so
strange to the Yorkshire lad as he pursued his way. Everywhere he was surrounded by crowds of dark-eyed,
enigmatic, unsmiling Chinese. Coolies swung along with
baskets dangling from both ends of the poles slung across
their shoulders, gasping out sing-song warnings as they
wound their way through the throng. Pig-tailed men
lounged in the open-fronted shops and restaurants that
lined the narrow streets. Vendors of steaming, savoury
foods stood by their little portable stalls, ready to provide
a meal at a moment's notice. Every now and then the
crowds pressed back to make room for a sedan chair
carried by running coolies, only to swarm into the street
again when it had passed. Hudson was to become so
accustomed to such scenes in the years that lay ahead that
they became as familiar as the Market Square at Barnsley;
but on this, his first day in China, it all seemed unreal,

almost fantastic. It was with a sense of relief, mingled with some apprehension, that he arrived at last at the large double gates of the Mission Compound.

A Chinese doorkeeper, hands tucked in his sleeves, bowed to the young westerner.

"Master wantee who?"

Hudson produced his letter of introduction and asked to see Dr. Medhurst.

"Doctor not at home. Doctor gone away." The gatekeeper, respectful but remote, bowed apologetically.

"Where has he gone?" asked Hudson. But the gatekeeper apparently had exhausted his stock of English. He just did not understand.

Here was a predicament indeed! It was already evening, and before long it would be dark. Alone in a strange city, unable to speak a word of Chinese, what was he to do? He tried again to make the gatekeeper understand, but without success, and he was on the verge of giving up when, to his relief, he saw a young man who was obviously a European walking across the compound. Hudson lost no time in introducing himself.

"My name is Edkins," said the young man pleasantly. "Dr. Medhurst is not here, but his colleague is, and I am sure he will be glad to help you. Please come in and sit down, while I go and fetch him. . . ."

That night, when Hudson eventually went to bed, it was neither in the bunk in his little cabin on the *Dumfries*, nor in some Chinese inn amongst people whose language he could not understand, but in a comfortable, clean bed in a large, airy room on the London Missionary Society Compound.

CHAPTER EIGHT

BESIEGED CITY

THE three young missionaries sat down somewhat wearily, though cheerfully, in one of the native junks drawn up by the muddy river bank, and mopped their faces as the boatmen pulled away from the shore. It had been a full day for them. Setting out from Shanghai after breakfast, they had arrived at Woosung Island about noon, and from that time until now had been distributing tracts, and talking as best they could with their limited knowledge of Chinese to the boatmen along the shore. The junks that plied the waterways around Shanghai were innumerable. Large and small, new and old, housing families whose whole lives were spent in their little floating homes, they had attracted the attention of Hudson Taylor and his friends, Edkins and Quarterman.

"We really ought to go and tell them about Christ," they decided. How could the poor idolaters with their little god-shelves and sticks of incense turn from idol worship and superstition if they never even heard of the One True God? So they had embarked on a day's missionary activity among them, glad enough to be free for a few hours from the grind of language study. Very well pleased with themselves they were now, as they relaxed at last, lulled by the gentle lapping of the water on the sides of the boat. The junk dwellers they had met had been friendly and willing enough to receive the neat little booklets handed to them, written in their own language. Some had even assured the young missionaries that having read them themselves, they would pass them on to others, at the ports to which they were going. It had been a day well spent, and now, as evening drew on, could they but get past the Chinese Imperial Fleet safely, they would be back in Shanghai before dark.

The problem was whether they *could* get past the Imperial Fleet safely. The boatmen were decidedly apprehensive about it, and not at all pleased that the three honourable gentlemen had left it so late to return. It was comparatively safe for native junks to cross the waters during the daytime, but to float around after dark, under the very noses of the Imperial guns, was a different matter. The Imperial guns had a habit of going off with very little provocation indeed, and anything seen moving on the waters after dark was liable to be suspect as belonging to the Rebels. It was altogether too late to be setting out on the return journey, and the boatmen did not like it. Even the missionaries were feeling slightly uneasy.

"If they know we are English and American, it will be all right," said Hudson. As belonging to the neutral Western Powers, whose warships were at anchor in the harbour, and whose armed men were ready to protect their life and property should they be assailed, they could move about in comparative safety. "But how are they to know, when it is dark?" How indeed? White skins and light hair could not be seen after dark. Only their voices could betray that they were not Chinese then. Only their voices. . . . Suddenly Edkins had an idea.

"I know!" he said. "We'll sing. We'll all sing together, at the tops of our voices in English, and they'll know we are Westerners." A good idea! Their throats were somewhat dry and strained, for they had already sung and talked a lot that day, in the course of their missionary activities, but they did their best, and as they approached some ships that appeared to be the Imperial Fleet they started going through their repertoire. Lustily they sang together all the hymns that they could remember, thankful to observe that they were passing ship after ship without being challenged.

They were just lapsing into silence, the last ship having been passed, when the boatmen said urgently, "Again sing! Again sing!"

But why? They were only now approaching the Imperial Fleet, they were told, the ships they had just passed were harmless cargo boats! "Quick! Quick! Sing! Sing!" hissed the boatmen.

" 'The spacious firmament on high'," gasped Edkins, and burst into song forthwith, the other two accompanying him. Over the waters three young voices floated, proclaiming sturdily that " 'the blue ethereal sky, the unwearied sun, the moon, and the stars that round her burn, in reason's ear they all rejoice, and utter forth a glorious voice, for ever singing as they shine, The hand that made us is divine.' "! It took three verses of eight lines each to advertise it adequately, and the last line was sung over twice, which certainly helped to spin it out. But alas! They reached their triumphant conclusion just as they were passing the largest ship in the fleet! "The hand that made us is divine" was followed by silence, as the three songsters sat breathing somewhat heavily after their exertions. And then, from the Imperial vessel was heard the ominous sound of an alarm gong being frantically beaten!

"What next?" cried Edkins. "We must go on singing. There's not a moment to lose!" and without waiting for a suggestion he started singing again. Simultaneously Hudson commenced singing something else, while Quarterman, evidently inspired by the situation, struck up, "Blow ye the trumpet, blow!" to a rollicking tune! The effect of the musical medley on those who listened was not reassuring! The men on the warship shouted, the panic-stricken boatmen yelled explanations, and for a few moments all were shouting something different at the tops of their voices. The Imperial Fleet, expecting some Rebel treachery, prepared to repel any attack. And the missionaries, realizing that the guns were in all likelihood being trained on them, heard an authoritative voice from the ship demanding, "Who goes there?"

"Great English Nation!" chorused Hudson and Edkins in reply.

"Flowery Flag country!" boomed Quarterman, the American.

"White devils! White devils!" yelled the boatmen. "White devils on board!"

"Where going?" came from the Imperial ship.

"Shanghai."

"Doing what?"

"Preaching their religion. White devils preaching their religion," explained the boatmen. This singular announcement might have been expected to produce panic, but strangely enough, it had the reverse effect. The Imperial Fleet grasped the situation. The boat was permitted to proceed.

"What do you mean by calling us white devils?" demanded the missionaries as they drew away from the fleet. "We may be white, but we are not devils," they said severely. "We are men of flesh and blood, created by the One True God, as you are. Devils are without bodies, and cannot be seen. Furthermore, they are evil spirits, enemies of the One True God, full of wicked intent towards mankind. Devils indeed! Surely you can see we are not devils but men like yourselves!"

The boatmen were very contrite, the more so as they

had not yet received their money. They had grossly offended the three honourable lords, they said. They had been greatly afraid when the commander in the ship had begotten such a fierce temper, and did not know what they were saying. Also, they were but low and uncultured fellows, and could not read a single letter, never having been to school. The exalted countries from which the honourable lords emanated were places of great learning and wisdom, unlike the poor and despicable land to which they had now come. They, the unworthy boatmen, had been greatly enlightened since the honourable lords had condescended to sit in their poor vessel and speak words of priceless wisdom. Never again, they asserted, under any amount of pressure, would they ever refer to the eminent and exalted ones from the Great British Nation and the Flowery Flag Country in such a way.

The missionaries tried to explain that they were not offended, only anxious that they should be recognized as human beings who had come to them with a message from the One True God. They parted on the shore on the best of terms, and that evening, as the boatmen squatted down with bowls and chopsticks to consume their evening meal of steamed rice, they agreed that the white devils were really very artless and harmless, and if somewhat unreasonable, at any rate they were generous with their money.

Hudson hurried away as quickly as possible when they landed, for he was afraid he would not be in time to cross the creek to the native city where he was living. Indeed, he arrived just as the last plank of the drawbridge was being withdrawn, and returned to his home tired, hungry, but happy. Sitting down in his little white-washed room he tackled his evening meal with zest. It comprised a bowl of steamed rice, and four little plates of Chinese vegetables and chopped meat, eaten with chopsticks instead of with knife and fork. Already it seemed quite natural to eat that sort of food in that sort of manner, and Hudson did good justice to it before going to bed.

It was nearly a year since he had set sail from Liverpool on the *Dumfries*. For the first few months after landing in Shanghai he had stayed in the hospitable compound of the London Missionary Society, where he had employed a Chinese man to teach him the language. Now, however, he had left the comfortable security of the International Settlement, with its Consulates and guards of well-armed European and American soldiers, and was living alone in a ramshackle native house near the North Gate of the Chinese City. He was constantly within the sound and sight of fighting, and the misery and suffering around him were appalling. Whole houses had been destroyed by gunfire, many poor people were homeless, beggars seemed to swarm the streets with their pathetic cries for "Bread! Bread!" It was no unusual thing to see captured soldiers being dragged along by their pigtails to be beheaded, or to hear their screams as they were tortured. The street in which he lived was one which the Imperialists had threatened to burn, and every night Hudson went to bed realizing that he might have to jump up and flee for his life before morning came. He always saw that his swimming belt was properly blown up before he went to sleep, for in the event of a sudden attack, he decided he would jump with it into the creek, and swim across to the International Settlement.

It was an eerie feeling to be alone in the upper rooms of the old house, with its innumerable passages and outhouses, in such circumstances, and many a time he would turn to his Bible to read some comforting passage before kneeling to pray. As he did so, however, he found that his fears were calmed. It was as though the strong, reassuring Voice of a protecting Presence spoke to him, and he went to sleep as peacefully as he had when he was a child with his mother telling him a story until he sank in slumber.

In spite of the constant danger, and the poverty and sorrow which surrounded him, he was happier now that he was actually living right among the Chinese people than he had been with other Europeans in the Settlement. There was a deep satisfaction in being able to do something to help these sufferers in their distress. His medical knowledge was already coming in useful, and better still, he was now able to talk Chinese a little, which meant he could speak about God, and His Son, Jesus Christ. He employed a Chinese Christian to run a little day school for children, and with this man Hudson went out into the narrow streets with their overhanging balconies and ornate swinging signs, distributing tracts and talking to such people as were disposed for conversation. Yes, he was beginning to do the very work he had come to China to do, and the thought of having to leave it saddened him. Yet he realized that he would probably have to do so. The fighting was drawing nearer almost daily, and the Rebel cannons were now at the end of the very street in which he was living, in preparation for defending it against the Imperialists. Had he had only himself to consider, he might well have decided to remain on and face what was coming. But he had received word from the Chinese Evangelization Society that they were sending out another worker, for whom Hudson was expected to make preparation—Dr. Parker who was already on his way to Shanghai with his wife and three small children! To bring another man to live with him in this dangerous place was one thing—to bring a mother with helpless little children here was another. Unless the situation improved, Hudson knew he would have to move back to the Settlement.

One night, having slept for a few hours, he was awakened with a start by the sound of a crackling and a roaring, and by a strange light reflected in his room. It was a fire! Amongst those wood-built houses, one joining another in the narrow street, a fire spread rapidly, as he knew, and in less time than it takes to tell Hudson was out of his bed and bundling into his clothes. There was a wind blowing, to make matters worse, and the dull red glow reflected in his room seemed to be growing brighter. He decided to climb up on the roof to see just where the fire was, and to his horror he saw it was apparently only a few houses away. In addition, he heard the all-too-familiar sound of shooting, and even as he looked around from his vantage point on the tiles, bullets splattered on the buildings around him. He crouched lower, his eyes still fixed on the fire. He could see the spirals of smoke and flames spurting over the curved roofs, and hear the sounds of excited talking and shouting in the street. What was actually happening he could not see, but he prayed silently and urgently that his Heavenly Father would protect him.

Even as he was praying drops of rain began to fall, and the wind dropped. Then a cannon-ball struck the roof of the house opposite, and fragments of the tiles flying past him, it dawned on him that his present position was neither safe nor comfortable! He climbed back into his room once more, thankful that the rain was falling more steadily, and the wind had dropped. The fire gradually subsided, and at five o'clock in the morning, realizing that the immediate danger was past, Hudson crept back into bed, to sleep for an hour or two before commencing the work of the day!

Shooting and fighting in the locality was almost a

nightly occurrence now, however, and there was nothing for it but to procure a home for the Parkers and their three children in the International Settlement. After many a fruitless search in the overcrowded area, he was eventually able to rent three rooms on the first floor of one of the houses in the London Missionary Society Compound. He was only just in time. Two days later the Parkers arrived, and Hudson, aged twenty-two, after barely eight months experience in China, found himself responsible for a family!

CHAPTER NINE

RIVER JOURNEY

THE Parkers were strong, sensible Scots, and prepared to put up with inconveniences and hardship. It was well that they were, for they very soon discovered they would have to! Three upstairs rooms in a rather small house might have proved adequate accommodation for them had the three rooms been suitably furnished with beds, cupboards and chests of drawers. Unfortunately, they were not. All Hudson seemed to possess in the way of furniture was a Chinese bed, two tables and half a dozen chairs. These, of course, were placed unreservedly at the disposal of the family, but Mrs. Parker looked round in vain for somewhere to put clothes, shoes, bottles and books. Alas, there were not even any shelves! Furthermore, there were no carpets on the floor, the windows were curtainless, and although it was winter, there was no fire!

It was, to say the least of it, rather a cheerless place after a long and uncomfortable sea voyage, for the family with three small children to come to, and poor Hudson, when he saw what the rooms looked like piled up with boxes, baskets and bundles, was overwhelmed with shame and confusion. He had not realized it would be as bad as that! But even if he had, it would have made little difference to the result. The fact was that after paying the first instalment of rent, he had less than three dollars left. He devoutly hoped that Dr. Parker would be adequately supplied with funds, for otherwise he was not at all sure where next week's food would come from. It was distinctly disconcerting, therefore, to learn that his new colleague only had a few dollars, and was expecting to find money awaiting him in Shanghai. The Chinese Evangelization Society had assured him they would send him some there.

No money was awaiting him however. Letters there were containing greetings and advice, but no mention of funds. As Hudson had already discovered, the financial arrangements of the Chinese Evangelization Society were extremely haphazard. There seemed to be an unexpressed conviction on the part of its leaders that when missionaries had run out of money, they could happily and healthily live on air until such time as more money was sent to them!

Fortunately, this view was not shared by the firm of agents who transmitted the Society's funds. When they realized the predicament Hudson and his newly-arrived colleagues were in, they lent them money until they should receive funds from the proper quarter. Thankful indeed was Hudson for this timely help—nor did he entirely disagree with the few tart comments the agents made about the business arrangements of the Chinese Evangelization Society! Indeed, he wrote the Society a frank though respectful letter himself, containing a few stiff phrases about their responsibilities to their missionaries, and then settled down as best he could, to accommodate himself to his new conditions. For the next few months he lived with the Parkers, and heartily glad he was to have such earnest and self-sacrificing fellow-workers as as they proved to be. Living with a family of five in three rooms was not conducive to quiet concentration on studying one of the world's most difficult languages, however. Many times did he think wistfully of the ramshackle house near the North Gate of the Chinese city, where he had constant contact with the Chinese themselves. That was the way to get to know them, to learn to speak as they spoke; to *live* amongst them. He was, therefore, delighted when his friend Edkins made a suggestion to him one day.

"I'm going to take a trip down to Ka-shing" he said to Hudson. "I shall hire a native house-boat for about a week and travel slowly, stopping at the towns and cities we pass to give out tracts and do some preaching. Will you come along with me?"

Would he! Hudson required no persuasion. To travel inland for a week, to live on a Chinese boat, to see Chinese life at first hand—this was the very thing he longed for! Forthwith he made his preparations, and quite considerable they needed to be—bed-clothes, baskets of food, fuel, a cooking stove, saucepans, as well as his medicines and a large assortment of books and tracts. As he walked down to the crowded shore behind the coolies he had hired to carry his baggage to the boat, he marvelled that so many things were required for so short a time! And what a bargaining and a shouting and a scrambling before everything was safely on board, and the boat drew away at last, winding its way between the innumerable junks anchored by the shores, into mid-stream! By this time, however, Hudson was getting used to the customs of coolies, and was not unduly perturbed when they yelled at each other, hurling epithets which he mercifully did not understand! They usually parted as affably as if they had merely been making enquires about each other's health, he observed, and evidently it was all in the day's work!

And now the boat was sailing along the broad waterway. Hudson gazed at the low-lying shore with its muddy banks and squalid-looking shacks, until gradually the scene changed as they drew away from the city towards the open country. Village after village they passed, and great tracts of land where innumerable mounds in the ground marked the graves of generations past. How thickly populated this country was, thought Hudson, as he looked at those shores. Little groups of houses clustered together every mile or two, and everywhere could be seen the signs of human habitation. When they eventually arrived at the first city where they were to go ashore, they were immediately surrounded by swarms of the blue-clad sons of Han, staring with undisguised interest at the two foreigners. Grasping as many tracts and booklets as they could conveniently hold Hudson and Edkins made their way up the bank and into the city.

It was while they were there, in that first city on their trip, they saw something which lived long in Hudson's memory. They had entered the courtyard of a temple, with its dragon ornamented roof and its gloomy halls where enormous, fearsome looking idols looked down impassively on the worshippers who bowed before them. The crowd that gathered around them listened quietly enough as Edkins and Hudson preached in turn, and when they had finished they had no difficulty in disposing of all the booklets they had with them. They were just about to move on when two or three of the priests, clad in rather dingy yellow robes and with clean-shaven heads, approached them.

"Honourable gentlemen, please come inside and sit down for a while," they invited politely, leading the way into their own living quarters. The two missionaries, interested to see the inside of a Buddhist monastery, accompanied them willingly. After a short conversation, the priests offered to show them around, and then said,

"Would you like to come and see our holy man?"

"Our holy man?" Who and what was he, the missionaries wondered? Yes, they said. They would indeed like to see the "holy man."

They were led to a remote part of the monastery, and

up to a wall. In the wall was a small opening, just large enough for a man's hand to pass through.

"He is in there," said the priests. Hudson looked for a door, but saw none. "There is no door," he was told. Almost incredulously Hudson realized that whoever was in there was *bricked in*! Peering through the opening he could discern but dimly the figure of a man, huddled against the wall. There was no window, so the only light that entered was that which made its way in from the gloomy hall. There he was, a human being like himself, alone in that tiny room which was indeed his coffin. He still breathed, and ate and drank the food passed to him through the hole in the wall, but apart from that, he might have been dead. In the dimness and the silence he passed his days and nights alone. By so doing, by cutting himself off from the fellowship of his fellow creatures, would he not crush his sins, would he not achieve holiness and accumulate much merit, as every natural desire was stifled? Certainly his religion taught him so, and he was already an object of great veneration in the city. Quite voluntarily he had entered upon the living death, believing that thereby he would attain Nirvana, the "heaven" of the Buddhists.

Edkins and Hudson exchanged significant glances. They had heard of these holy men, poor devotees of a heathen religion but had never before seen one. Moved by a feeling of deep compassion, Edkins drew near to the hole, that he might the better speak to the man inside. He had come to him with a message from the One True God, he explained, and very earnestly he told the "holy man" that his sins could be freely forgiven, for Christ's sake. As clearly as he could, Edkins spoke of Jesus on the cross, and of His rising again from the dead, to be the Saviour of those who trusted in Him. But it was all strange and new to the man in that bricked-in wall, and to the yellow-clad priests standing around. Never had they heard this "foreign religion" before, and they gazed at the two missionaries with dark, impassive eyes, and politely disbelieving faces. They had their god—Buddha. The Westerners evidently had their god—Jesus. Good, good. It was all good. It mattered not what religion it was, all led to the way, they said. They accompanied their two visitors to the gate of the temple courtyard, bowed affably, and returned to the dark building with its fitfully flickering oil lamps, its incense sticks and fearsome idols, and its "holy man" in his dark stillness.

Hudson and Edkins emerged into the street, and almost immediately became the centre of attraction again. They had to return to their boat two or three times to obtain further supplies of tracts, and on one occasion narrowly escaped being trapped on the water's edge by the crowds that swarmed around them. It was not until evening was drawing on that they had an opportunity to be quiet, and review the happenings of the day. Climbing up the winding stairs inside a pagoda, they stood together looking down silently on the scene below. The city looked like a lake of roof-tops from their high vantage point, and they could see across them to the stout, solid walls encircling it and the flat countryside beyond. The paddy-fields, profusely sprinkled with clumps of trees that betokened the presence of villages, stretched right away to the horizon. Here and there pagodas and temples with curved roofs standing out against the sky told of other cities and towns not far away. Hundreds of thousands of human beings were living within the range of their vision, they realized, as they stood watching the evening shadows lengthen over the innumerable dark little homes with their idols and their paper gods, their incense sticks and their ancestral tablets. And this was only on the very fringe of the great heathen Empire that stretched away for hundreds of miles into the unexplored interior.

The interior, Inland China. As Hudson stood in the pagoda that evening, the immensity of China's population began to have a new meaning for him. Shanghai with its narrow native streets and teeming markets had more or less bounded his vision hitherto, although he and Dr. Parker had walked many times miles out into the country to preach and distribute tracts in the villages around. Now, however, looking over the great silent plain, he became dimly aware of regions away towards the west, great tracts of land where cities, towns, markets and villages lay in a profusion that defied the imagination. And in them all, the only Way the people knew was the dark way of death. He remembered that silent, walled-up man in the monastery. . . . The temple gongs, the worship of ancestor spirits, the fear of demons—like a pall they seemed to hang over this great Eastern civilization. It seemed to be lying hopelessly in the arms of some immense, evil monster. The boy who had heard a Voice saying "Go for Me to China" began to comprehend as never before the greatness of the task before him. And perhaps, as never before, his very soul steeled itself for the battle. Here was a conflict that was going to demand every ounce of his strength, that required courage and determination above anything he had imagined. It was in a solemn frame of mind that he returned to the boat that evening. Whatever it cost, however rough the way, the people of this land must be told of the Only One who could save them from death.

CHAPTER TEN

ABANDONED IN CHINA

HUDSON sat down wearily on the temple steps, and decided he would have to spend the rest of the night there. It was already past one o'clock in the morning, and he had searched in vain for a place to sleep in the unfriendly city. All doors seemed closed against him, and he was too exhausted to walk any more. He stretched himself out on the cold, uneven stones, put his little bag of money under his head, and wondered if he would be able to sleep.

With his long blue gown, cloth slippers and, above all, a clean shaven head from the crown of which dangled a long pigtail, he looked as much like a Chinese man as a fair-skinned, blue-eyed Yorkshire youth could possibly expect to look. Months ago he had taken the step of dressing exactly as the Chinese did. He had called down a good deal of criticism on himself from fellow-Europeans as a result, but he was able to mingle much more freely with the Chinese themselves, and had travelled extensively in places where most Europeans would have been mobbed. This was the first time he had ever had to sleep out of doors. But somehow, things seemed to have been going all wrong lately. First there was the fire which had destroyed all his medicines—a serious loss, for they would be very expensive to replace. Then there was the disappearance of his servant and all his luggage two days ago, leaving him stranded with nothing but the clothes he was wearing. And now, there was the crowning misfortune of being unable to find a lodging. Well, when day broke he would have some breakfast, make a final search for the missing servant and luggage, and then return to Shanghai. It would be futile to attempt to reach Ningpo, where the Parkers were now living, with the small amount of money left in his possession. He pressed his face into his hard, knobbly pillow, sighed sleepily, closed his eyes. . . .

Suddenly he was wide awake, his body tense but motionless. What was that moving in the darkness? A dim figure was coming stealthily across the wide steps towards him, and Hudson, still lying as though asleep, discerned the ragged form of a beggar. The man crept silently to the form of the recumbent missionary, and stood looking down at him. Hudson did not move, and after a minute or two, evidently assured that he was asleep, the beggar bent down and began gently feeling him.

"What do you want?"

Hudson spoke quietly enough, but there was an ominous ring in his voice! The beggar was taken by surprise. The man lying there wasn't asleep after all—indeed, he sounded very much awake, as though he were prepared to take immediate action! The beggar beat a hasty retreat.

Hudson decided his money should be in a safer place than under his sleeping head, so having put some of it in an inner pocket, and the rest up his sleeve, settled down again. He was just dozing off when some instinct once more aroused him. He was conscious of movements in the darkness, the dim outlines of silent figures approaching. The beggar had returned with a companion or two! Again Hudson lay motionless until he felt a hand moving behind his head, feeling for the bag of cash.

"What do you want?" he asked in the same quiet but significant tones as before. He received no answer, but the beggars retreated a couple of steps, and sat down.

"What are you doing?" demanded Hudson.

"Spending the night here outside the temple—like you," came the reply.

"Then kindly go over to the other side, and leave me here," said Hudson. "There is plenty of room for you there."

The men made no reply to this suggestion, but did not move. Hudson therefore sat up. It was useless lying there, where he might drop off to sleep. He would certainly be robbed of all he had left unless he kept his wits about him.

"You'd better lie down and sleep," said one of the beggars, disarmingly, "or else you'll not be able to work to-morrow. Don't be afraid," he continued reassuringly. "We shan't leave you. We'll see no one does you any harm!"

"You listen to me," said Hudson stoutly. "I don't want your protection. I don't need it. I am not a Chinese, and I don't worship your useless idols. I worship God, He is my Father, and I trust in Him. He will protect me. I know what you are, and what you intend doing. I tell you, I shall *not* go to sleep. I intend keeping my eye on you."

The beggars did not move, and neither did Hudson. Sitting with his back to the wall, trying not to nod off to sleep, the hours passed slowly. Every now and then he made a remark, partly to make the men realize he was still awake, and partly to help himself to remain so! Eventually he hit on the idea of keeping himself awake by singing, and when he got tired of that, repeated passages of Scripture aloud, and then prayed. These devotions did much to cheer him, while having exactly the reverse effect upon the beggars, who grumbled to each other, urged him to be quiet, and finally departed altogether! Just before dawn, seeing they had disappeared down the narrow street, Hudson relaxed at last, and even slept for a little while ere the city began to stir.

"Foxes have holes, the birds of the air have nests; but the Son of Man hath not where to lay His head." The words had a new meaning for him that day, as he trudged along the track between endless rice-fields on his way to the place where he hoped to get on a boat going to Shanghai. His Master knew what it was to be despised and rejected, as he had been the previous day when searching in vain for a lodging. His Master knew what it was to suffer the cold and discomfort of sleeping out of doors, and to be dogged by unscrupulous men. How insignificant seemed his own sufferings and humiliations compared with all that Jesus Christ, the Lord of Glory, had endured for him. How little it mattered if he had lost all his belongings, as certainly appeared to be the case. The souls of these Chinese people were of infinitely more value than his cherished earthly possessions. Why had he worried so much about them, and cared so little about the souls of these poor, ignorant, sinning people? "Oh, Lord," he prayed as he walked along, "forgive me for all my short-comings. Help me to do only Thy will, help me to follow in Thy footsteps. . . ." Nothing else mattered much, but to follow in those footsteps, and to become more like his Master.

That night he was invited by friendly boat-people to sleep on board with them, and glad indeed he was to do so. It was cold without his bedding, but it was a relief to lie down without fear of being robbed. He got up the next morning with a sore throat but a light heart, for all anxiety about his losses was gone. After all, God was well able to restore them to him if that would be for the best, and if not, then he did not want them!

Now all that remained was to find a boat going to Shanghai, and return there forthwith. He would search for his servant and his luggage no more. He set out on the long walk to the town where he hoped to find a boat, and after paying for the breakfast he had in a little wayside inn, he found he had only eight hundred and ten cash left. It would be just enough to pay his fare and provide him with food for the three or four days it would take to reach Shanghai. Now to find a boat to take him there as soon as possible!

But there was no boat going to Shanghai. There was not even one going as far as Ka-Shing Fu, he was told. Hudson tramped from boat office to river bank, enquiring of any likely individual whether he knew of a boat going in the direction of Shanghai—all in vain. The boats were grounded in the dry river bed, and until rains came and the waters rose, there they must remain. It might be weeks before they could move—and he had only money enough to last about five days! Hope seemed well-nigh gone when suddenly he espied a mail boat, smaller than the heavy cargo junks that lined the river bank, making its way along the narrow stream that still flowed in the middle of the bed. It was going in the direction of Ka-shing Fu!

"Hi!" Hudson started running, weariness and sore feet forgotten. The boat was ahead of him, and he tore along for a mile before he was in earshot.

"Are you going to Ka-shing Fu?" he yelled.

"No!" was the reply.

"Are you going in that direction?"

"No."

"Will you take me as far as you *are* going that way?" asked Hudson in desperation.

"No."

Hudson stopped dead, watching the boat go on. This

was the last straw! He felt sick, and a wave of coldness seemed to sweep over him.

"Better sit down," he thought, and sank down on the grassy river-bank, suddenly faint. Then everything went blank.

How long he lay like that he did not know. Gradually he returned to consciousness, and as he did so he heard the sound of voices. They came from the other side of the canal, and as he came to himself he realized they were talking about him.

"He speaks pure Shanghai dialect," someone said—in pure Shanghai dialect! They evidently took him for a native of their own city. The next thing he knew a small boat was coming across the water to fetch him, and he was invited to come on board.

The kindly junk-people heard his story sympathetically. His servant had disappeared with his luggage, he himself had been searching for two days, and now he had only sufficient money to take him back to Shanghai—and there was no boat! They looked pitifully at the weary Westerner who was dressed as they were, and spoke their language like a native. And when, after he had drunk some tea, they gave him warm water to wash his feet, it was with little exclamations of surprise that they saw how blistered they were. But his troubles were at an end. The captain of the junk gave him food, then found a boat going to Shanghai and offered to pay the fare himself, if necessary. The tide of misfortune had turned at last.

On his arrival back in Shanghai Hudson set on foot enquiries about the servant who had disappeared with his luggage—£40-worth of it! Had the man met with difficulties himself—been arrested, perhaps by some unsympathetic official who did not approve of Chinese who worked for Westerners? Or had he just made off with the

stuff himself? It was not long before it became apparent
that the latter was the case, and Hudson was strongly
advised to have the law on him! Such a man ought to be
punished, he was told, and Hudson agreed in theory.
However, there was another point to be considered. He
had many times preached to his servants of the love of God,
of the forgiveness which the Lord Jesus Christ shewed even
to those who nailed Him to the cross. Here was his opportunity to demonstrate that spirit of forgiveness himself, by
returning good for evil. Instead of putting the case into
the hands of a Chinese mandarin, therefore, he wrote his
servant a letter, pointing out the wrong he had done, and
urging him to change his ways. How much more import-
ant it was, thought Hudson, that the man's conscience
should be touched, that he should turn to God and his
soul be saved from hell, than that *he* should get back £40-
worth of baggage! If only this act of forgiveness would
have that effect on the man, how willingly would Hudson
be deprived of twice the amount he had lost—if he *had*
twice the amount which, in point of fact, he had not!
Having despatched the letter, he set about selling what
sticks of furniture still remained to him in order to make
up as best he could the indispensable possessions he had
lost, before setting out once more for Ningpo.

Just as he was preparing to leave, news came that a
mail-boat had arrived from England. The arrival of a
mail-boat was always hailed with joyful anticipation by
the European community, and Hudson was as eager as
anyone else to collect the letters that he hoped would be
awaiting him at the agent's office. He had to endure a few
supercilious glances from top-hatted gentlemen who had
also arrived to collect their mail, and who viewed the
pig-tailed Englishman in Chinese clothes with undisguised scorn. He was getting accustomed to that! He

received his letters, and returning home eagerly scanned them. Would there be one from his mother, or Amelia, with news of home and Barnsley? Would there, by some good chance, be one from the Chinese Evangelization Society containing his salary? Or one from his friend Ben, perhaps, to say he wanted to come and join him in the work?

Ah! Here was one in a hand-writing that was becoming familiar. It was from Mr. Berger, a man who had grown very interested in the work of the young missionary, and whose friendly letters always breathed a warm encouragement that cheered Hudson's heart. He opened it, and read until he came to the words:

"Please accept the enclosed as a token of love from myself and my dear wife." The enclosed—what was it? Hudson opened out the little slip of pink paper tucked inside the letter and saw with amazement that it was a cheque made out to him—for £40. Hudson just stared at it.

There it was again! Another tangible evidence that God knew all about his affairs. He had lost £40-worth of baggage, and here was the money to replace it—sent out from England at least six weeks before he had even been robbed! (He little knew then that another such sum was soon to be on its way from someone else, too!) How glad he was that he had taken no steps to have his servant punished for stealing his things. And as he set out again through the beautiful province of Chekiang, with its orchards and steep little hills, its willows and its paddy-fields, he felt like a boy who had passed another examination, and heard the ring of commendation in his master's voice as he said, "Well done!"

CHAPTER ELEVEN

MISS ALDERSEY'S EARTHQUAKE

MISS ALDERSEY was a wonderful woman. Every-one in Ningpo agreed about that, Chinese and Westerners alike. Indeed, the Chinese regarded her as being of far greater importance than the British Consul who, they asserted, invariably obeyed her commands. And no wonder! Was she not endued with magical powers? Were not the earthquake tremors which recently occurred due to the fact that she had opened a mysterious bottle containing a potent charm at five o'clock one morn-ing on the city wall? And were not other strange phenom-ena also due to the Honourable Teacher Aldersey's occult power? No doubt the Queen of England, a remarkable woman herself, had appointed her to rule those of her subjects who had gravitated to the Chinese port city of Ningpo. Of course the British Consul obeyed her! Yes, said the Chinese, Miss Aldersey was a wonderful woman.

The European community thought so too. While they did not attribute the earthquake to her, knowing full well that her bottle contained nothing more devastating than smelling salts, they felt that she did something more noteworthy than that every day of her life. At five o'clock in the morning, winter or summer, wet or fine, she went for a walk on the city wall. It mattered not to her if it were pitch dark. She merely instructed a servant to accompany her with a lantern, and sallied forth as usual for her daily constitutional. At five o'clock in the morning! It would have required more than a mere earthquake

tremor to induce the European community to do likewise! Yes, if for that feat alone, they agreed she was a
wonderful woman. But that was not all. The pioneer
woman missionary in Ningpo, founder of the first Protestant school for girls in China, she had a capacity for work
which left frailer mortals breathless. She would listen to
her pupils reading their lessons to her even while she was
eating her meals. And as for holidays, she would none of
them. Other missionaries might go off to the seaside to
regain health and strength after their exertions, but Miss
Aldersey got the sea breezes by climbing to the ninth
storey of a tall pagoda, and sniffing them from there.
Some of her pupils accompanying her, she was thus
enabled to continue imparting knowledge to them un-
hindered. A remarkable woman, without doubt, and if
the British Consul did not always do exactly what she
wanted, he certainly would not have dared to let her
know!

It was most unfortunate for Hudson, therefore, that
such an influential and awe-inspiring person as the
admirable Miss Aldersey should have taken a deep,
strong and rooted dislike to him. Such, however, was the
case. The very mention of his name was sufficient to
stiffen her frail little body with what she considered
wholly righteous indignation. For Hudson Taylor had
actually had the temerity, the audacity, the unmitigated
effrontery, to propose to Maria!

Maria was the orphan daughter of a missionary, and
she was one of the teachers in Miss Aldersey's school. A
very useful little teacher she was, too, fond of children,
and speaking Chinese like a native. She was rather pretty,
and Hudson was not the first young man who felt that the
name Maria would look better in front of his surname
than in front of her own. However, Miss Aldersey did not

hold that against her, for after all, the girl could not help it. To give Miss Aldersey her due, she was quite prepared to part with her attractive, efficient young teacher if a really suitable man appeared on the scene. But Hudson Taylor! That young man who always wore Chinese clothes *and a pigtail*! A pigtail of his own hair, mark you, dangling from the crown of his head! Who was he, any-how? A poor, young, unconnected Nobody! A fanatic, completely undependable, whom no reputable missionary society would ever employ! Marry Maria? Never! He was merely after her money!

Poor nineteen-year-old Maria was overwhelmed. As far as her own feelings were concerned, the idea of marry-ing Hudson, pigtail or no pigtail, appealed to her strongly. Truth to tell, it had occurred to her several weeks before Hudson had even mentioned it, although, needless to say, she had kept it to herself. Now, however, in the face of Miss Aldersey's wrath and powerful reasons, she felt helpless. At that lady's dictation she sat down and wrote a curt letter to say that the proposal was wholly im-possible, adding that if Hudson had any gentlemanly feeling at all, he would never again refer to the subject. Miss Aldersey took the letter off in triumph, Maria went to her room and burst into tears, and Hudson, who had expected a more favourable reply, felt as though a door had been slammed, loudly and finally, in his face.

It was not easy to settle down to live and work in Ningpo after that rebuff, but Hudson knew that he must do so. He had already obtained possession of a shop which made an excellent preaching-hall, and was living, not with the Parkers, who were in charge of a hospital but with a young couple, Mr. and Mrs. Jones, who had recently arrived in China. Hudson's days were full, preaching, visiting Chinese who were inquiring about this

"Jesus religion" and doing medical work. It was well for him that they were. He was very lonely. His hopes of companionship all seemed to crash, one by one. When first he came to China he had hoped that before very long his sister Amelia would come and join him. He was fond of Amelia, for all his teasing, and felt she would have been just the one to run the home for him, and work among the Chinese women. Then he had been encouraged by letters from his friend Ben, who was evidently deeply interested in his experiences. Perhaps *he* would come! It was somewhat of a shock, therefore, when he received the news that Amelia and Ben had got engaged, and were settling down at home, so *neither* would be coming. Now that Maria who, it must be admitted, he had felt would make an even better companion than either of them, had turned him down, he was bereft indeed.

The days of early summer, therefore, were not without their sadness for him. He was perplexed. He had prayed a great deal about the matter before he had gone so far as to propose to Maria. It was strange that things should have taken the turn they had, when he had felt convinced he was doing the right thing. And somehow, try as he would, the feeling that it was the right thing still persisted. He would have been quite certain about it, had he been able to hear poor little Maria's daily prayers, as she knelt by her bedside, morning and night! She very much wanted to be Mrs. Hudson Taylor!

Hudson, however, knew nothing about that. All he had to go on was Maria's letter, and that had been final—apparently. Certainly, he knew he was intended to regard it as such, but the more he thought about it, the more he felt he couldn't. It was her writing, but it was not her way of putting things. He began to wonder if it was not more like Miss Aldersey's way of putting things. . . . If only, thought Hudson, it were possible to see Maria when Miss Aldersey was not around. But in old China, where custom forbad an unmarried man to try to meet an unmarried woman, his hands were tied. Their paths rarely crossed. The one effort he had made to talk to her misfired, and he found himself left with someone else, while Maria was whisked away in a sedan-chair! Eventually he decided there was nothing he could do about it. His pigtail dangled disconsolately through the hot, sticky June days, as he went about the narrow streets, and preached for an hour or so each evening in the "Jesus Hall". He could not but realize that were he to cut it off, he would be regarded as being a much more suitable match for Maria. But if he cut it off, it would mean he could no longer move about freely among the Chinese, who regarded him almost as one of themselves. And he knew why he had heard that Voice "Go for Me to China". There was a work for him to do in this land, and that work was to spread abroad the knowledge of the only One who can save from eternal death. There were towns and cities, villages and hamlets lying in the interior, that were waiting for that News, and he must go. . . . The pigtail must remain. But as Hudson knelt by his bedside, night and morning, praying for the Chinese, the name of "Maria" was also mentioned with fervent supplication, before he rose from his knees.

And then, quite suddenly in the middle of July, the whole situation was changed by a waterspout.

It was an amazingly well-timed waterspout. It came sweeping up the river one afternoon when Mrs. Jones was entertaining all the lady missionaries in Ningpo in her home. It broke over Ningpo in a startling deluge, followed by torrential rain. In no time all the streets were running with water and emptied of people. Water poured off roofs and formed ponds and pools in unexpected places, and the ladies looked out of the windows of Mrs. Jones' drawing-room and wondered how and when they would get home again. It was indeed much later than usual that some sedan-chair carriers eventually arrived at the front gates, their trousers rolled up over their knees, and water dropping from the wide brims of their coolie hats. And even then, there were more ladies than sedan-chairs. So, naturally, some ladies had to stay behind, while some were carried home. Amongst those who were carried home was Miss Aldersey. Amongst those who still awaited sedan-chairs was Maria. And there she was when Hudson and Mr. Jones arrived home from the preaching hall!

A smallish drawing-room in which three or four people are sitting is not considered an ideal place for a proposal of marriage, especially from someone who has already been rejected. Hudson realized that, and his first intention when it dawned on him that here at last was Maria without Miss Aldersey, was merely to ask politely if he might write to her guardian in London for permission to cultivate her acquaintance! However, once he started, he found himself saying more than that, in spite of onlookers. And Maria, usually rather quiet and reserved, responded with surprising and encouraging warmth! In a remarkably short time the position was made quite clear. When the sedan-chairs arrived to convey the remaining ladies through the muddy streets to their homes, no one in the drawing-room was left in any doubt as to how matters stood. Young Hudson Taylor had Maria's full permission and approval to write to her guardian. And although no such sentiment was expressed in words, it was evident to all that not even one of Miss Aldersey's earthquakes would prevent him doing so!

*　　　　　*　　　　　*

Although Hudson wasted no time in writing to Maria's guardian, it was over four months before he received a reply, for his was not the only letter that the mail-boat carried from Ningpo to London addressed to Mr. Tarn. Miss Aldersey wrote to him, too! Mr. Tarn felt it necessary to make a few discreet enquiries from people in London who knew Hudson before committing himself, but when he had done that he decided that if his niece and ward wanted to marry this young missionary with a pigtail, there was no reason he knew of why she should not do so. He merely stipulated that as she was now already over twenty, she should wait until she came of age before taking the step. Less than a year after the occasion of the waterspout, therefore, Hudson and Maria were married and had settled into the attic over the preaching chapel in Bridge Street.

Bridge Street, Ningpo, was as suitably named as Drainside, Hull, had been, for it was a narrow thorough-fare which started with a bridge and ended with a bridge. As one of them spanned a canal, which ran along at the back of his home, Hudson had plenty to remind him of the old days. He had first taken up his abode in this attic when he was a lonely bachelor, and one morning had awakened to find it covered with a thin film of snow, which had drifted in through the tiled roof during the night. He had waited long enough to trace his initials on the coverlet before he stepped gingerly out of bed and got dressed! However, he decided that the place probably needed doing up a bit before he could bring Maria there, so when she arrived, as Mrs. Hudson Taylor, it was to find it partitioned off into four or five little rooms, all of which had ceilings! And there, living right among the Chinese, dressing as they did and speaking their language, they settled down to their work.

CHAPTER TWELVE

CHINESE CONVERTS

MR. NEE, looking tall and dignified in his well-cut silk gown and wide-sleeved jacket, walked slowly along the narrow street. The coolies, with their rough straw hats and sandalled feet moved to one side as they saw him approaching, for he was obviously a man of learning, one who could not only read, but understand, the Classics. As such, he was entitled to the respect of the ignorant and unlearned. Those who recognized him knew also that he was a well-to-do businessman, and for this reason, too, the poorer people stood aside. Mr. Nee moved easily along the street with its flagged pathway and its wide, double-leafed doorways, musing on the uncertainties of life, and still more on the uncertainties of death. What, he wondered, happened after death? The mystery that shrouded the Dark Unseen disturbed him, making him apprehensive and uneasy. Where was the Way, the Truth that would bring relief and enlightenment to his perplexed mind?

The clanging of a bell attracted his attention, and he turned to see from whence the sound came. One of the double-leafed doorways stood wide open, and as Mr. Nee looked into the courtyard, he saw several people walking across it, and into the door of a long room. It looked as though some sort of meeting was about to commence.

"What are they doing in there?" he enquired of a street vendor, standing by his little portable stall.

"That's the Jesus Hall," came the reply. "Foreigners

live in there. When they ring that bell, then they do their worship."

"What do they do when they worship?" asked Mr. Nee.

"They sing, and read from their Sacred Classics, and then explain what they've been reading."

Mr. Nee looked again at the open doorway, and decided to go in. He would investigate this foreign religion. Perhaps it would explain some of the dark mysteries of life and death. He entered the room, sat down on one of the benches, and looked towards the little raised platform where a young man was standing, reading aloud from a book he was holding in his hands.

At first sight, the young man appeared to be a Chinese, for he was dressed as such, and only his light eyes and white skin betrayed him. But Mr. Nee was not so much interested in the young man as in what he was reading, and he listened intently to the story of a conversation a Teacher called Jesus had with a man who came to see him at night.

"As Moses lifted up the serpent in the wilderness, even so must the Son of Man be lifted up; that whosoever believeth in Him should not perish, but have eternal life. For God so loved the world, that He gave His only begotten Son, that whosoever believeth in Him should not perish, but have everlasting life. For God sent not His Son into the world to condemn the world; but that the world through Him might be saved."

Everlasting life. That was what Mr. Nee wanted. Not to be condemned, but to be saved. He sat in the preaching hall that evening, gripped by what he heard. This Jesus, whom the foreigners worshipped, was God's own Son. He had come from Heaven into the world as a Man, had died upon a cross, when He bore the sins of all the world, and after He had been dead three days, He came to life again. He came out of the tomb. He walked and talked with His friends, and then one day He left the earth and went back to Heaven. He would give Everlasting Life to all who believed in Him.

So this was the Way! Sitting in that little preaching hall, with its rice-paper windows and rows of wooden benches, Mr. Nee knew without any doubt that this was the Way. Something within him responded unquestioningly to what he heard. His sadness and perplexity departed. When Hudson closed his Bible and ceased preaching, Mr. Nee rose to his feet. All eyes were turned to him as he said, with quiet, oriental gravity:

"I have long sought the truth, as my father did before me, without finding it. I travelled far and near, searching for the Way, but never found it. In the teachings of Confucius, the doctrines of Buddhism and Taoism, I have found no rest. But I have found rest in what we have heard to-night. Henceforth I am a believer in Jesus."

And he was as good as his word. He explained quite simply to his friends why he would worship and burn incense to the gods no more. He obtained a Bible and commenced studying it, attended the meetings in the little preaching hall, and accompanied the missionaries practically every day when they went out preaching and visiting. He was not the first Chinese who had turned from idols to the Living God after hearing Hudson preach, but none, perhaps, had turned so clearly and definitely on the first hearing of the message.

"How long have you had this Good News in your honourable England?" he asked Hudson one day.

Hudson hesitated. This Chinese gentleman, who had responded so gladly and readily to the loving invitation of the Living God was so eager that others should hear it too!

"Several hundred years," said Hudson, rather reluctant to have to admit it was so long.

"Several hundred years!" exclaimed Nee in amazement. "Is it possible that in your honourable country you have known about Jesus so long, and only now have come to tell us?" In his mind's eye he saw a man he had loved, earnestly reading the Classics, eagerly going to the temples to prostrate himself before the still, unresponsive idols, sitting in silent thought and meditation, seeking to understand the mysteries of life and death, a sadly wistful expression on his face.

"My father sought the truth for more than twenty years," he said slowly. "And he died without finding it. Oh, why did you people not come sooner?"

*   *   *

Through Mr. Nee's enthusiasm in speaking to all he met about Jesus the Lord, Wang the basket-maker also became a believer. A cheerful, impetuous man was Wang, and he went forward on the Christian pathway not without a tumble or two! But his sincerity was evident. He had been accustomed to working seven days a week, of course, like everybody else around him, until he joined the Christians. When he heard, however, that the Living God had ordained that one day out of seven should be set apart as a day of holy rest, he obeyed the command without question. It meant his employer did not give him any food, nor yet the princely salary of twopence which was paid him for each day's work, although he was expected to accomplish as much in his six days as he had previously done in seven! But Wang the basket-maker felt himself well repaid for his sacrifice as he sat in the Jesus Hall on Sundays and listened to the amazing stories from the Holy Book. And when his irate employer, during the busy season, informed him that if he wouldn't work for him on Sundays he couldn't work for him at all, Wang decided that he must look for employment elsewhere.

On Monday morning, therefore, he visited another basket-maker, to try and find another job. No, he was not wanted. He went to another, with the same result. He tramped around the city in vain. Although they were all so busy, none of the basket-makers would employ him. And Wang came to the conclusion that the devil was making things hard for him because he was determined to worship, instead of work, on Sundays.

"I must resist him," thought Wang. He was not prepared to take that sort of opposition lying down, for Wang was a man of some spirit! "I will resist him! If he won't let me get other employment, then I'll give my time to plucking souls from his kingdom!" He made no further efforts to obtain employment, but took a bundle of tracts in his hands, and sallied forth into the street to talk to any men he could find who were willing to listen to him preaching about Jesus! And that was how he met Wang the farmer.

Wang the farmer, some time previously, had had a remarkable experience. He had been lying alone in his home in the little village of O-zi, seriously ill, when he heard a voice calling his name. Knowing none of his family were in the house, he clambered slowly from off his big, four-poster bed, to go to the door. No one was there. He lay down again, when for the second time he heard his name called. Once more he dragged himself to the door, only to find no one there. Thoroughly frightened, he cowered under the wadded coverlet on his bed. Surely, he thought, this was the voice of the King of Hell, come to warn him that death was approaching!

Then he heard the voice again, and it told him not to be frightened, for he was not going to die. He was going to get well! And when he was well, he was to go to the city of Ningpo, thirty miles away, where he would hear of a new religion. This religion, the voice said, would bring him peace of heart.

To everyone's surprise, Wang the farmer *did* get well! And remembering his instructions, he went to Ningpo. Having got there, however, he searched in vain for the new religion. No one seemed to have heard of it. For several weeks he lived in the city, earning his living by cutting grass and selling it to people who had cattle to feed, always hoping to hear of the religion that would bring him peace of heart. But it was not until the Monday when he encountered Wang the basket-maker that he found it.

Wang the basket-maker was sitting in a tea-shop, talking eagerly to a group of men who were in there sipping tea. He was talking about a God whom he called Jesus, who could forgive sins, when Wang the farmer came in and sat down. However indifferent the other listeners may have been to the preacher's message, one at least was spell-bound! Oblivious to the buzz of conversation that came from the men who lounged in bamboo chairs around the little tables of the tea-shop, deaf to the cries of the street vendors and the coolies passing up and down the narrow street outside, Wang the farmer had ears only for what the man at the next table was so eagerly telling those who were sitting with him. Forgiveness of sins, and a free entry into Heaven for all who came to this God, Jesus—was not this the new religion that would bring him peace of heart?

Wang the basket-maker and Wang the farmer left the tea-shop together. They spent the evening poring over the New Testament, and Wang the farmer was told that he must go to the Jesus Hall, where the foreign teacher would explain to him still more concerning this Jesus religion. Wang the basket-maker went to bed that night with the knowledge that he had indeed snatched a soul from the devil's kingdom!

He obtained employment early Tuesday morning. The very first basket-maker to whom he applied took him on without hesitation. Wang soon discovered the reason for this sudden reversal of fortune. His former employer, angered by his refusal to work on Sundays, had notified all the other basket-makers, who belonged to the same society as himself, not to employ Wang if he came round on Monday looking for work. On Monday, therefore, Wang searched for employment in vain. But now it was Tuesday, not Monday, and that was quite a different matter. It was the busy season, Wang was a good basket-maker, and whatever his former employer had *meant*, he had certainly only *said* Monday. Any of the men who had turned Wang away the previous day, would willingly have taken him on Tuesday.

It was not long after Hudson had been introduced to Wang the farmer that Wang the basket-maker arrived one day at the Jesus Hall with another man. This time it was a painter, whom he had met in the courtyard of a wealthy family where he had gone to sell baskets. The ladies of the house, standing around him on their tiny, bound feet, wanting little baskets to keep their incense in, had enquired with some annoyance why he refused to make them. The single-hearted Wang explained that as a believer in Jesus, the True God, he could have nothing to do with idols, the incense that was burned to them, nor yet the baskets in which the incense was kept. The ladies had listened to his strange Jesus doctrine for a while, then, tiring of it, had turned back into the house. He was gathering up his baskets to carry them off the premises when a young man, dressed in coolie clothes, suddenly appeared before him.

"What was that you were saying?" demanded the stranger. "You didn't see me—I was up there, painting." He pointed to a ladder that leaned against the wall, under a gaily-coloured overhanging roof. "What was it you were saying? I heard—but tell me again!"

Wang needed no second bidding. The painter listened again to this surprising news of a Living God who desired to save, not to punish, erring men, and when it was suggested that he should go to the Jesus Hall to learn more, he readily agreed.

Hudson smiled and bowed at the new arrival. Wang the basket-maker was certainly a good fisher of men! It was only a short time ago that he had brought along Wang the farmer, and now this one! He looked into the dark, earnest eyes of the young working man before him, and asked politely,

"What is your honourable surname?"

"My despicable surname," came the answer, "is Wang."

CHAPTER THIRTEEN

LAUNCHING A MISSION

WANG the painter shuffled along the narrow passage of No. 1, Beaumont St., Whitechapel, and opened the front door. In his loose-fitting Chinese clothes, his skimpy pigtail dangling down his back, he looked strangely out of place against the background of a rather dingy little house in a London side-street, and the young man standing outside the door suppressed a start of surprise when he saw him. It had not occurred to him that the missionary from China whom he had come to see would have brought a Chinese servant back with him.

"Is Mr. Taylor at home?" enquired young Meadows.

"Pleese come in" said Wang in his soft, pidgin English. "I go see master. . . ." and in a minute he returned to show the visitor into a small, barely-furnished room. Hudson was sitting there, engrossed on the task that had occupied him since he had returned from China a few months previously, and which was likely to prove a long one—the revision of the New Testament in Chinese. His pigtail had gone, now that he was back in England, and in his old, well-worn suit he looked like a poor clerk who could not afford to keep a good fire burning in the grate. Cold though the day was, it was nearly out! Young Meadows' quick eyes took in the apparent poverty of the man he had come to see, and who was rising now, a bright, welcoming smile on his face, to greet him. And when, later, he sat down to a simple dinner with Hudson and Maria, and observed that the table-cloth was distinctly grubby, and the food, cooked by Wang, was not up to standard, he might well have felt discouraged at what he saw of the life of missionaries. But as a matter of fact, he was not discouraged at all. These two young people, both under thirty, who could tell him such tense and thrilling stories of besieged cities, escapes from pirates, and who had such wonderful answers to their prayers, made a very deep impression on him. It was evident that they had a purpose in life. It did not matter to them if their clothes were old-fashioned or their carpets had holes. They simply were not concerned about clothes and carpets. What absorbed them was the realization that millions of Chinese knew nothing about the true God, and therefore they *must* be told. And young Meadows who felt the same way about it, and wanted to go to China to tell them as soon as possible, decided that Hudson was the missionary society he would like to join!

Hudson had to explain that although he was most eager that people should go to China to spread the good news that God loved man, and hoped to return there himself soon, he was really not in the position to be a missionary society, as he had no money! He had not enough to send even one missionary to China. Actually, since he had returned to England, a very sick man, he had rarely known from where next month's rent would come. He had long since left the Chinese Evangelization Society, and was so busy completing his medical training and revising the Chinese New Testament that he had no time to "work for a living". It was remarkable how the money came in, sometimes in the very nick of time, from friends and relatives who were interested in him, and in China. He realized that it was God who moved them to do it, and his faith in his Heavenly Father increased greatly. All the same, he felt he was in no position to employ missionaries, in the circumstances, and said so.

Young Meadows, however, felt otherwise. After all, if God could move people to support His servant, Hudson Taylor, could He not also move people to support His servant, young Meadows? At any rate, inspired by what he had seen and heard, he assured Hudson that he was willing to go to China on the assumption that God would.

And so Hudson obtained his first missionary, who sailed for China a few months later. Remembering his own early experiences in Shanghai, Hudson determined that his missionary should receive money and letters regularly, not spasmodically. He bought a large, important-looking account book, in which he made careful entries of money received and transmitted it to young Meadows very promptly. He also bought a file to keep letters in, and wrote often. After a year, young Meadows' only cause for complaint was that he was so well looked after, and received money so regularly, that he sometimes felt he was not living by faith in God at all! He seemed quite disappointed at not suffering hardship through shortage of money! Hudson replied that he had no idea where his next month's salary was coming from, or how much it would be, and that they must continue praying to God for supplies. Young Meadows was reassured!

But what was one more missionary in a land where millions upon millions of people were living and dying without once hearing of the Only True God? There was a large map of China hanging on the wall of the little study in 1, Beaumont St., Whitechapel, and Hudson's eyes constantly roamed over it as he lifted them from the Chinese and English Bibles on the desk before him. He read over and over again the names of provinces far away from the coast. Such musical, picturesque names they had, that stirred the imagination—South of the Clouds, Four Streams, West of the Mountains, North of the Lake,

Clear Sea, South of the River. . . . Protestant missionaries had never penetrated into those distant places, and Hudson thought of the hundreds of cities, the thousands of towns, and the tens of thousands of villages they contained. Hundreds, thousands, millions. . . . It was the thought of the millions that continually oppressed him. Millions of Chinese people—lovable, erring Chinese people, like Mr. Nee, and Wang the basket-maker, and the farmer from the village of O-Zi. He was reminded of the Chinese people every day as he looked into the face of the faithful painter Wang, who had left home and country to serve him. And then he remembered the monk who was walled into a cell in the temple, hoping to find "the Way". He thought of Mr. Nee's father, who had sought "the Way" for twenty years, and died without finding it. And the more he prayed that God would send missionaries to those far-away provinces, the more he felt he ought to do something about it himself.

He had already approached all the missionary societies he could think of, to urge them to send men to inland China—to those vast provinces with the picturesque names, where millions of people were still waiting to hear of Jesus. He had been listened to sympathetically enough, but told that nothing could be done at present. And the thought came again and again that he ought to start a missionary society himself, to go to those remote inland regions West of the Mountains, South of the Clouds, North of the Lake. . . .

He studied the map on his study wall long and earnestly and often. There were eleven great provinces, and the mysterious country of Tibet, with no missionaries. If only, thought Hudson, there were but two missionaries for each province! That would, at any rate, be a start.

"Then why don't you ask God to send them to you?"

It was a most unwelcome thought, and Hudson did not like it. He did not *want* to start a missionary society to go to inland China. He was quite prepared to go there himself, but he did not want to send other people. Supposing when the young men and women sent by him got there, insufficient money was received to support them? Supposing they died of starvation? Or supposing the Chinese were angry at people coming to preach a different religion, and killed them? All sorts of horrible possibilities came to his mind. How terrible, thought Hudson desperately, to have been the one to send them to their death! The responsibility was too great, he felt, and he tried to put away the thought of starting a missionary society. But he could not. There it was, and there it remained.

It was on a Sunday morning in June, on the beach at Brighton, that he finally decided he would have to do it. Walking slowly over the pebbles down to the water's edge, he looked across the calm, sunlit sea with his mind in a turmoil. Fancy being responsible for sending men and women to the far-off, unknown regions of inland China, where perhaps they might die of starvation! On the other hand—fancy leaving those millions of Chinese to die without knowing of God! That was far more dreadful. And then, quite suddenly, it occurred to him that even if the missionaries did all die of starvation, well, they would go straight to Heaven—and what could be better than that! And if, before they died, they had turned only one Chinese from worshipping the devil to worshipping God, it would have been worth it. This somewhat pessimistic reflection, strangely enough, made him feel quite a lot brighter!

Then another thought occurred to him. If he did start a missionary society to go to the inland of China, it would

only be because he knew that God was urging him to do
it. And if God was urging him to do it, then all the
responsibility for what happened would be God's, not
his!

Now why, thought Hudson, had that not occurred
to him before? God would be responsible, not he! As this
realization sank into his mind, he felt as though a great,
crushing load was being gently rolled away.

"Oh, Lord!" he prayed with a tremendous sense of
relief. "Thou shalt have all the burden!" It had gone
already—no longer was he oppressed by the thought of
starving missionaries! "I will go forward as Thy servant,
at Thy bidding. . . ." Yes, he must start a missionary
society, and now he knew he could. All fears of what
might happen in the future had dissolved like a morning
mist before the sun. What happened as a result of obeying
God's Voice was not his responsibility. All he had to do
was to go forward, asking God to send what was necessary
to start a missionary society to go West of the Mountains,
South of the Clouds, North of the Lake. . . .

Eleven provinces and Tibet, thought Hudson. There
should be two workers for each, to begin to take the good
news of God's love to Man to the interior of China.
Twice twelve are twenty-four. So Hudson, standing
bare-headed on the beach that Sunday morning, closed
his eyes. He stood like that for several minutes, the waves
lapping at his feet. Then he opened his Bible, and made a
note in it. "Prayed for twenty-four willing skilful labourers
at Brighton, June 25, 1865." and walked light-heartedly
over the pebbles to the promenade where full-skirted
ladies strolled with top-hatted gentlemen, and sprightly
horses trotted between the shafts of coaches and pony
traps. But Hudson had no eyes for the fashionably dressed
people thronging the sea front. His thoughts were very

far away. Twenty-four workers, including Maria and himself, to take the good news to the millions in Four Streams, South of the River, Clear Sea, North of the Lake. . . .

He never doubted but that God would answer his prayer. Nor did it trouble him that he, who had barely enough money to support his wife, and family, would now begin to require an income of thousands of pounds a year to support the twenty-four willing, skilful labourers. If he was doing God's work in God's way, God would certainly send in the money required!

Hudson was very practical. The workers and the money would be provided, were probably already on the way! He must prepare for them. He returned to London on Monday, and on Tuesday he paid a visit to the bank.

"I want to open a new banking account," he told the manager.

"How much have you to start with?" enquired that official.

"Ten pounds."

"And whose name is the banking account to be in?"

"The China Inland Mission," said Hudson.

The missionary society was launched!

CHAPTER FOURTEEN

DESTINATION—INLAND CHINA

HUDSON walked along a broad street in the West End, near Regent's Park, and mounting the wide steps of one of the large houses, rang the bell. The door was opened almost immediately by a manservant, and not without a feeling of shyness Hudson entered a well-furnished hall, very different in appearance to the narrow passage that led to the front door in 1, Beaumont St., Whitechapel!

"Her ladyship is expecting you," he was informed, as he handed the butler his hat and stick. And then he was shown into the room where he was to take breakfast with the Dowager Lady Radstock.

It was less than a week since the launching of the China Inland Mission, and Hudson was scarcely prepared for the direction in which things were moving. He was not accustomed to moving in the circles of high society! But his hostess, whom he had met for the first time at church the day before, put him entirely at his ease. She wanted to hear about China, and as he told of those millions in the inland provinces, and how God was urging him to go to them, not only she, but others at the breakfast table were interested. In a surprisingly short time he was receiving invitations to attend luncheon parties with titled people, and to speak at drawing-room meetings where all the guests appeared in evening dress! As the weeks sped by he found himself carried along as though by a full tide, travelling not only in England, but in Scotland and Ireland, too, to meet people who had heard about his enterprise, and to speak at meetings, large and small.

At one of those meetings he met a bright and witty young man who was later to become the founder of the well-known Dr. Barnardo Homes. At that time Tom Barnardo was only twenty, and a member of the theological class to which Hudson had been invited to speak. Quite a diminutive young person was Tom Barnardo, and when he observed how short and slight the missionary from China appeared beside the tall, well-built figure of the class leader, he whispered to his next-door neighbour, "Good! There's a chance for me!" For he, too, wanted to go to China, and appproached Hudson about joining the Inland Mission. It was on Hudson's advice that he embarked first on a medical training at the London Hospital, where he discovered that his vocation was the rescuing of waifs and strays in England, after all. But he was by no means the only young person to be stirred to action on hearing of the needs of the Chinese people West of the Mountains, North of the Lake, South of the Clouds. . . . Hudson had prayed for twenty-four skilful, willing workers on that memorable Sunday morning on the Brighton Beach, and God was answering that prayer.

The days were never long enough for Hudson now. Travelling, speaking at meetings, interviewing people who wanted to join the Mission, writing booklets about China, he went from one task to another with never a stop, it seemed. There were seven or eight missionaries already in China, including young Meadows, who were eager to join the Mission that was to go to the inland provinces. And as 1866 dawned it became evident that his twenty-four skilful, willing labourers had already been given—for sixteen young men and women were prepared to sail with him and Maria to China as soon as arrangements could be made to do so.

The arrangements that needed to be made, of course, were largely of the type that require money. Hudson reckoned that it would cost nearly £2,000 to get him and his party to China, and by the first week in February he had only £170 in hand. And they hoped to sail in May! It did not appear very likely that they would, in the circumstances. But somehow Hudson felt sure that God was going to send them in all that was required. He and Maria decided they would hold a prayer meeting in their house every day at twelve o'clock, to ask Him to do so, and to pray for His direction and help in all connected with their going to China. Once more he proved how very practical it is to pray! Within five weeks of commencing that daily prayer meeting all the money they needed had come in. One man alone had given £650! Now all that remained was to find a sailing ship on which the whole party of eighteen adults and four children could be accommodated.

That was not so easy, it seemed. April passed into May, and still no suitable sailing ship bound for China was procurable. Nevertheless—Hudson and his party were still hoping to sail in May.

On May 2nd, Hudson was in Hertfordshire, staying in the home of a Colonel Puget, who had invited him to speak at a meeting about his work. It was what is known as a "good meeting." So earnestly and quietly did the audience listen as Hudson spoke of the millions in China who had never heard of Jesus, that the proverbial pin might have been heard to drop. And Colonel Puget, the chairman, felt it was too good an opportunity to let pass. Hudson always stipulated that there should be no collection taken up at any of his meetings, but Colonel

Puget felt this meeting should be an exception. Why, the people were obviously deeply moved—undoubtedly they would give most generously toward the work of the new China Inland Mission if the plate were but passed around! He was somewhat provoked, therefore, when Hudson restrained him as he was about to announce that there would be a collection.

"You made a great mistake, if I may say so," he said at supper. "The people were really interested. We might have had a good collection." Indeed, although he did not say so, he himself had intended putting £5 in the plate! This enthusiastic young missionary leader was too impractical! His ideal of only asking God for money was splendid, but to refuse to allow a collection at a meeting where people were obviously eager to give seemed to be carrying things too far. So thought Colonel Puget as he retired to bed.

Strangely enough, he could not get to sleep. As he lay in bed, turning from one side to the other, his thoughts went back to the meeting. Hudson had spoken most movingly about the Chinese who were dying without once having heard of the Only One who could save them. "Every hour a thousand of them die, going out into the darkness of an Eternity without Christ. . . ." Every hour a thousand. . . . Every hour a thousand. . . . The thought of it seemed to burn into the very heart of the good Colonel. All thought of the wasted opportunity of taking up a large collection was gone, as he seemed to see the broad stream of Chinese going steadily, hopelessly into the darkness. Something must be done to let them hear that there was a Saviour! Something *was* being done, of course. That gallant little band of labourers! Mere youths and maidens, most of them, prepared to sacrifice their lives if need be, to follow young Hudson

Taylor right into the heart of that great Eastern Empire.

"But what can *I* do?" thought the elderly Colonel, and his thought became a prayer. "Lord," he prayed earnestly, "what wilt Thou have *me* to do?"

He remembered the £5 note he had intended to put in the plate as a donation, and somehow it seemed pathetically small. In the darkness the Colonel prayed again. "Lord, what wilt Thou have me to do?" After a long time he fell asleep—but when at last he did so, he knew what he must do.

The following morning, before the Colonel put in an appearance at the breakfast table, the postman had delivered a letter to Hudson from a firm of shipping agents. A ship called the *Lammermuir* was about to sail for China, and Hudson was offered the entire cabin accommodation for his party. It sounded just what was needed—would the price asked be beyond their reach?

The Colonel appeared, explaining that he had had a bad night, and apologizing for being late, and they sat down to breakfast. When it was over, the Colonel asked Hudson into his study.

"I have some money here for you," he said, handing him several contributions that had been given him to pass on to Hudson. Then he continued:

"I felt last evening that you were wrong about the collection, but now I see things differently. Lying awake in the night, I thought of that stream of souls in China, a thousand every hour going out into the dark. I could only cry, 'Lord, what wilt Thou have me to do?' I think I have His answer," and he handed Hudson a cheque. "If there had been a collection I should have given a £5 note," he added. "This cheque is the result of no small part of the night spent in prayer."

Hudson looked in wonderment at the slip of paper in

his hand. The cheque was made out, not for £5, but for £500!

There was no question now as to whether he could afford to book the entire cabin accommodation of the *Lammermuir*! The unexpected cheque, coming right on the heels of the notification of the sailing vessel seemed to be God's assurance that it was the boat on which he and his party should travel. And on the *Lammermuir*, less than a month later, they set sail for China—the first of a steady stream of men and women that for more than eighty years poured in to the great cities and numberless villages of the regions West of the Mountains, South of the Clouds, North of the Lake, to tell men like Mr. Nee, and Wang the basket-maker, and the farmer from O-Zi, about Jesus. . . .

Hudson leaned on the railing of the ship, looking out to sea. It was not yet a year since he had made that entry in his Bible "Prayed for twenty-four skilful, willing labourers at Brighton, June 25, 1865." How quickly things had happened since that day! It seemed as though God had just been waiting for him to take that one step, and when he took it, he found everything else was prepared.

The first time he sailed for China, a lonely youth of twenty, he had but vaguely realized the purpose for which he had been sent. "Go for Me to China," the Voice had said, and he had obeyed. This time, as a man of thirty-three, he understood more clearly the task that had been set him. He was to lead his little band of labourers into the very heart of China, to spread throughout the length and breadth of that great Empire the news of God's love to man.

That difficulties and dangers, hardships and heartaches lay before him he was well aware. It was no comfortable, easy task to which he was called, but a campaign that would demand every ounce of his strength and endurance. Nevertheless, he was not afraid. All that was required of him, after all, was loyal obedience to his Master, and unswerving trust in Him. Christ was the leader, not he, and with such a Leader he was prepared to follow to the end. It was with an eager, happy heart that Hudson, leaning on the rails of the *Lammermuir* as she ploughed her way through the waters, faced his life-work.

"I heard the call, Come Follow,
    That was all.
  Earth's joys grew dim,
  My soul went after Him.
    I rose and followed—that was all.
    Will you not follow if you hear Him call?"

CHAPTER FIFTEEN

AFTER FORTY YEARS

IT was forty years after the day on Brighton beach when he had finally decided to found the China Inland Mission, and Hudson was sitting in a mission station in South of the Lake. It was the last of the eleven provinces that had opened to his missionaries. Four Streams, North of the Lake, South of the River, West of the Mountains, South of the Clouds—one by one mission stations had been occupied in all of those inland provinces, but still the hostile officials of thickly populated South of the Lake refused to allow the Westerners with their religion of Jesus to settle there. For over thirty years Hudson had prayed for the door to open, and now at last even in South of the Lake the China Inland Mission had its workers.

Hudson looked out of the window across the roofs of the city to the distant horizon. It was his very last day on earth, although no one knew it yet. He did not know it himself. He was thinking more of the past than the future as he turned to talk to his companion.

"It is a wonderful privilege we have, to be able to bring everything to God in prayer, isn't it?" he said with a smile. This was one of the things that impressed him most. God had done so many of the things he had asked Him to do. Answering his prayer for twenty-four workers had only been one of them. Hudson had gone on praying for more missionaries, and God had gone on sending them. Twenty years ago he had prayed for seventy more, and God had sent them. Then, a few years later, he had prayed for another hundred, and God had sent them, too. Now there were more than eight hundred members in the Mission, scattered over the whole vast interior of China, in which not one province remained where Jesus was not preached. Many were the obstacles that had been encountered, yet sooner or later they had been overcome. Even now there were difficulties—there always would be —but Hudson knew that as he prayed, God would solve them all.

"A wonderful privilege—to be able to bring everything to God in prayer. . . ."

"Yes. . . ." The younger man looked across at the old missionary, and said slowly:

"You know, I sometimes feel I can't bring *everything* to Him. The big things—yes. But many things seem too small to pray to God about. The feeling that they are too small really hinders me from praying. . . ."

Hudson, white-haired and stocky, seemed almost surprised. "I don't know anything about that," he said. Too small to pray about? Some of the very small things in his life had led to very big things. Half a crown was not very much money, but giving away the last one he had, over fifty years ago, had started him on the path of faith and obedience; the prick of a pin was so small that he scarcely noticed it, yet it had almost cost him his life; a pigtail was really a very small thing—yet how large it had loomed when he was the first and only missionary to wear one! One of the shortest prayers of his life had been when he prayed on the Brighton beach for twenty-four skilful, willing workers, but had not that prayer started the Mission for Inland China? Who could say what was big and what was not?

"There is nothing small, and there is nothing great," he said, after a slight pause. "Only God is great." And then, as though summing up all the experience of the years, he added simply, "We should trust Him fully."

He went to bed very soon after that, for he was tired. It had been a happy day. In the morning he had gone to the chapel to speak to the Chinese Christians—men and women of South of the Lake, who had found "the Way." In the afternoon he had had tea on the little lawn in the garden, and met all the other missionaries in the city, who had come to visit him. He had enjoyed it all very much, but now he was tired, and thought he would not go downstairs for supper.

"We'll bring it up to you in bed," he was told, and he went into his room. Twilight fell over the city. The outline of the distant mountains faded into the darkness, and in the sky overhead the stars appeared. It was very quiet. After a time light footsteps were heard on the stairs, as the supper tray was carried up. The door of Hudson's room was opened, then there was silence again, followed by quickly running footsteps and a cry from the top of the stairs.

"Doctor! Doctor!" He came immediately. But as soon as he looked at the happy, peaceful face on the pillow, he knew he was not needed.

* * *

"Venerable Pastor, Venerable Pastor," whispered the young evangelist, bending over the quiet form on the bed, holding one of the old hands in his two warm ones. He had come in from an outstation that very day, in order to see the famous old missionary of whom he had heard so much. And now he must speak to him, even though his words would not be heard.

"Venerable Pastor, we truly love you. We have come to-day to see you. We longed to look into your face. We too are your little children—Venerable Pastor, Venerable Pastor. You opened for us the road, the road to heaven. You loved us and prayed for us long years. We came to-day to look upon your face.

"You look so happy, so peaceful! You are smiling. Your face is quiet and pleased. You cannot speak to us to-night. We do not want to bring you back; but we will follow you. We shall come to you, Venerable Pastor. You will welcome us by and by. . . ."

But Hudson had been welcomed already. As one of the Chinese women said as she looked at him, her eyes full of tears, but a smile on her face. "Ten thousand times ten thousands of angels have received him!" And above their welcome rang one Voice he had learned to listen for on earth, and which he loved beyond all others—the Voice he had heard, long ago, saying "Go for Me to China." But this time the Voice said, "Well done! Good, faithful servant! Enter into the joy of thy Lord!"

And Hudson entered.